Becoming Biliterate

Through the real-life example of Emma, one child learning to be bilingual and biliterate, this book raises questions and provides a theoretical foundation and a context for understanding and reflecting on the complexity by which young children learn to read and write in multiple languages as they actively construct meaning and work through tensions resulting from their everyday life circumstances. Highlighting the social and cognitive advantages of biliteracy, and opening a space to explore and discuss issues of language rights, *Becoming Biliterate*:

- addresses the complexity of writing across different writing systems
- examines the writing and drawing forms that result from one child's active discovery when she was allowed to explore written forms of English and Japanese
- situates written language as a cultural tool to raise the larger connection between writing and identity
- looks at the relationships between learning to read and identity through a code-switching lens
- describes what happened when Emma met the English-dominant world of school

Perspectives regarding identity and language ideologies are presented to help teachers refine their own pedagogical approaches to teaching linguistically diverse children. Reaction Questions and Suggested Activities in each chapter engage readers in articulating and questioning their own assumptions and beliefs, and in connecting what they are reading to their own experiences with multilingual children and/or classrooms.

Bobbie Kabuto is Assistant Professor of Literacy Education in the Department of Elementary and Early Childhood Education, Queens College, City University of New York.

Becoming Biliterate

Identity, Ideology, and Learning to Read and Write in Two Languages

Bobbie Kabuto

Routledge
Taylor & Francis Group

NEW YORK AND LONDON

First published 2011
by Routledge
270 Madison Avenue, New York, NY 10016

Simultaneously published in the UK
by Routledge
2 Park Square, Milton Park, Abingdon, Oxon OX14 4RN

Routledge is an imprint of the Taylor & Francis Group, an informa business

© 2011 Taylor & Francis

Typeset in Minion by
RefineCatch Limited, Bungay, Suffolk
Printed and bound in the United States of America on acid-free paper by
Walsworth Publishing Company, Marceline, MO

Library of Congress Cataloging in Publication Data
Kabuto, Bobbie.
    Becoming biliterate : identity, ideology, and learning to read and write in two languages / Bobbie Kabuto.
        p. cm.—
    Includes bibliographical references and index.
    1. Bilingualism in children.   2. Second language acquisition.   I. Title.
    P115.2.K33 2010
    404.'2083—dc22   2010004687

ISBN13: 978–0–415–87179–2 (hbk)
ISBN13: 978–0–415–87180–8 (pbk)
ISBN13: 978–0–203–84643–8 (ebk)

To Emma and Rick

So long as men can breathe or eyes can see
So long lives this and this gives life to thee.

William Shakespeare, Sonnet 18

Contents

Foreword

DENNY TAYLOR

Becoming Biliterate is a work of deep scholarship. It is a groundbreaking book that challenges current theoretical and pedagogical assumptions about young children's experiences of becoming biliterate. Equally remarkable to the erudition is the simple elegance of the writing. Bobbie Kabuto has the ability to present complex ideas with an almost effortless ease. The book is a page-turner, as good as any novel. But don't be deceived, eight years of disciplined systematic research on language, (bi)literacy, ideology, and identity undergird the text and make it possible for Bobbie to write with such authority and conviction. Her stance on literacy learning repositions not only researchers but also teachers and is of significance to the field.

She writes, "A new way of thinking about biliteracy is needed to encompass the notion that becoming Biliterate (with the big "B") is first and foremost learning to become someone in this world" (p. 4). The "someone" in Bobbie's book is her daughter, Emma. In many ways Emma reminds me of Lucy in *The Lion, the Witch and the Wardrobe* and later Alice—in Wonderland and Through the Looking Glass. Both Lucy and Alice are learning to become someone in the world but, however much instruction they receive, most of what they figure out is through their active engagement with those they meet in the world and the situations they find themselves in. Events and meaning are not separated, and so it is for Emma.

In *Becoming Biliterate* Emma is Bobbie's guide. Through close ethnographic observation and motherly engagement Bobbie is able to disambiguate the roles of using two languages in learning to read and write, and to see the cognitive, social, and emotional benefits of becoming biliterate. She then helps the reader to consider the complexities of the multifaceted processes of becoming biliterate. For some readers this will be an exhilarating experience as new perspectives expand, modify, and replace the old. For other readers the disequilibrium that these new perspectives bring will be challenging, and the desire will be to hold on to the status quo. But the opportunity will exist for teacher-educators and teachers to build new curricula and pedagogical practices to support bilingual/biliterate students, which are in keeping with the current movements in education that embrace commonsense notions of language, literacy, and schooling—which frame biliteracy and language rights for children and families.

Bobbie's deep scholarship as a parent researcher provides her with a unique opportunity to use multiple theories as she takes an in-depth look at Emma's experiences in becoming biliterate. She writes:

> It was through the experience of watching and raising my daughter Emma that I began to challenge the notion of what becoming biliterate entails and why languages other than English matter; why families matter; why children's rights matter. (p. xiii)

From this experience Bobbie advances the proposition of a "meta-language"—I think of it as the capacity for language that all human beings share, before the divisions. Bobbie explains, "Emma did not necessarily see language learning as language separation, in which she needed to separate languages depending on context. Instead, Emma appeared to draw on a variety of linguistic resources to communicate and construct meaning (p. 11). It is this revolutionary idea in language learning and teaching that creates a spot for Emma alongside Lucy and Alice. Clearly we have always known that we can learn from children, as these fictional characters in great novels make clear to us, but Emma is a real child whose experiences of becoming bilingual and biliterate deepen our sensitivities to the urgent need for us to build our theories of human learning upon what children teach us instead of the current practice of imposing our adult driven theories upon them.

Bobbie helps us see that as soon as Emma attempted marks on a page she was in the process of writing her own identity. In becoming biliterate, Emma's language and literacy engagement in the social and cultural contexts of her everyday life provided her with continuous opportunities to work through, and weigh up, the multiple ideological stances toward written and spoken languages that she encountered, and that were available to her. Through her active participation in her social world, she was able to create her own social and cultural identity—a social, cultural, and personal construction as original as "Emma." Here, the journeys of Lucy in Narnia and Alice down the rabbit hole or through the looking glass become analogous. In Emma's journey into her biliterate world she learns that certain languages and ways of representing are privileged over others, and she "lives out" these experiences in her writing—enacting her understandings in ways that Bobbie could systematically document and rigorously think about from the multiple theoretical perspectives that are central to her scholarship and study.

When Bobbie accompanies Emma on her journey, unsettling questions arise about schools and the ways in which misconceptions about language, literacy, and learning are reproduced and transmitted from one generation to the next. Other questions, just as unsettling, emerge about the ways in which language used in school and classroom settings might negatively realign home languages, even families and their values. Bobbie presents cogent arguments that deserve to be considered about the language lessons children learn in many schools which might at best be irrelevant and at worst counterproductive to becoming biliterate—especially in the ways in which families use language.

Preface

It was a familiar scene: the first day of the fall semester. Waiting for the elevator to take me downstairs to my "Introduction to Bilingual and Biliteracy Instruction for Children," a graduate student approached me and asked where Room 17 was located. I immediately introduced myself as her professor, and we made small talk until the elevator came. In the meantime, other students gathered, many of them recognizing each other from previous courses. The elevator opened. I moved to the back, toting my black crate filled with syllabi, books, and handouts, anxious, as I always am, about the first day of class. The line of students filed in, chatting openly. The graduate student who I met earlier started talking with another graduate student who asked, "Are you in this class too?"

"Yes," she replied, "Did you buy the books yet?"

"I'm not going to buy the books for this class. I can't believe that I have to take this class; it sounds so stupid," she said to the horror to her friend, clearly expressed in her wide open eyes and the slight nod of her head.

The elevator opened. I strolled out in embarrassment, not for myself, but for the student, for she would soon discover that her professor was keen to her feelings about taking this course. Upon her horrified revelation that I was the professor in the back of the elevator, I heard, "She's the professor!" I turned around and, giving my motherly warning, suggested that one should always be cautious of what one says in elevators and bathroom stalls. I had my work cut out for me this semester, I thought to myself.

This graduate student's comment was not surprising to me at the time as it represented many of the feelings of other students who have entered my classes each semester. Nonetheless, it was disconcerting and disheartening to see some teachers openly dispassionate and uninterested about a topic that I was so passionate about and that has affected my life and the lives of children across the nation: the language rights of bilingual and biliterate children.

General views around the irrelevance of language instruction for bilingual children, such as the one this graduate student held, come at a time when the national trend for foreign and native language instruction in schools is in a spiral decline. According to a 2008 National K-12 Foreign Language Survey conducted by the Center for Applied Linguistics (CAL), the overall number of elementary schools offering instruction in other languages has drastically fallen. Based on preliminary findings, the CAL reported that public elementary schools providing instruction in a language other than English decreased from 24% to 15% from 1997 to 2008, in spite of the fact that there was a 7% increase in foreign and native language instruction between 1987 and 1997. Out of programs implemented in elementary schools only 13% focus on immersion programs in which a native language is used 50% of the day with the goal of achieving English proficiency.

This trend counters a 2000 Census (US Census Bureau, 2006) which found that nearly one in five people aged five and over living in the USA reported speaking a language other than English in the home. Overall, the number of people speaking a home language other than English doubled between 1980 and 2000. Despite the fact that we are living in an increasing globalized world and, according to the Census, becoming a linguistically diverse society, we are building dams in the form of schools to block out the overflow of languages in our families and communities. It is time that the dam receives another crack in its foundation.

In many ways, this book is in response to the current movements in education and the commonsense notions of language, literacy, and schooling that are framing biliteracy and language rights for children and families. It adds to a whole body of literature that highlights the multifaceted processes that occur in becoming bilingual and biliterate (Compton-Lily, 2007; Fu, 2003; Hantzopoulas, 2005; Moll, 2004) and the extensive knowledge that bilingual and biliterate children acquire (Cummins, 1984, 1994; Krashen, 1982; Perez, 2004). At the same time, this book is unique. It was through the experience of watching and raising my daughter Emma that I began to challenge the notion of what becoming biliterate entails and why languages other than English matter; why families matter; why children's rights matter.

Becoming biliterate is a journey. Young biliterate children navigate through the unknown; they revel in their successes and sometimes wallow in their struggles. But it is always a journey of self-discovery and a way to reconcile differences of perspectives, opinions, and beliefs about language and literacy. In this book, I would like us to take Emma's journey together, the person who encouraged me to rethink both by theoretical and pedagogical orientations toward early biliteracy.

My Journey

My professional and personal journey to this point began in my personal life in 1998 with the birth of my daughter Emma. Both my husband Jay and I are bilingual and biliterate individuals who are able speak, read, and write in English and Japanese. Although I was raised in a bilingual home, I was not a proficient bilingual until college where I took classes to recapture my Japanese. Jay learned English also in college, but was raised in a Japanese-speaking home. Although we ended up in similar places, we took different paths to get there. We wanted something different for Emma; we wanted her to be bilingual and biliterate from the beginning.

Emma was born in Tokyo, Japan, in 1998. At the time, I was teaching second grade at a large international school in Tokyo. After Emma's birth, I took a year off from teaching to stay home with Emma; however, when I decided to go back to work, Emma, who was 1 year old at the time, went to the local Japanese day care in our neighborhood. Having spent only one year there, Emma does not remember much about her Japanese day care. In fact, she does not remember much about Japan from these early years other than knowing that it is the place where she was born.

I collected Emma's writing and drawing samples from 2 years until 7 years of age, which spanned a time from living in Tokyo to moving to New York and from working in an international school to attending graduate school. In addition, within that time, Emma's brother Ricky was born in 2003. Initially, my desire to save Emma's writing and drawing was in the attempt to save pieces of her early childhood experiences. But they evolved into critical data that documented Emma's early biliteracy, particularly when I entered graduate school and studied the complexity of children's pathways into literacy.

The evolution of written language forms in her writing and drawing was documentary data of her early biliteracy. For instance, my first collected drawing consisted of green, red, yellow, and pink lines that Emma made when she was 2 years, 1 month old. Slowly, I watched as these lines transformed into facial features and the letter *E* at 2 years, 11 months old. Three months later at 3 years, 2 months old, lines took on another evolution into the letter *M* and *A*, which formed Emma's name. Those same lines that formed the letter *A* became a Chinese character when Emma was 3 years, 6 months old.

In addition to collecting writing and drawing artifacts, reading also became of interest. Documenting Emma's movement into reading, I audiotaped reading events and conversations, and observed. Emma's reading and writing were interconnected; they supported each other. Emma was writing lines, shapes, alphabetic letters, and Japanese scripts before she was ever reading conventionally in either language. It seemed that the physical actions, the perceptual abilities, and the cognitive demand of making marks of a variety of forms created a foundation for her early reading and writing across languages.

When Emma was 1 year old, instead of returning to my second-grade classroom, I started teaching pre-kindergarten in an international school. I remember that I had a small class with very lively, outspoken personalities. Teaching in an international school was a challenge and, at the same time, a rewarding experience. Some students spoke as many as three languages: English (language of instruction), Japanese (language of the community), and a third home language. In the school where I taught, children who spoke only English received instruction in Japanese in order to develop both languages. Having very little theoretical and practical understanding of learning in multiple languages (I never took a class in bilingualism in my teacher-education courses), I faced the daily challenges of working with students who had a variety of language experiences and abilities in English and Japanese. But there was one experience that made me critically reflect on my role as teacher and children's rights to their languages.

This experience involved a 4-year-old in my pre-kindergarten class. His home was bilingual, like mine; his mother was bilingual in English and Japanese while his father could only speak Japanese. Yet, his speech was incomprehensible to the point that no one could tell which language he was speaking. Even after testing by a psychologist and speech therapist, no one could really find an explanation other than blaming his bilingualism. Similar to many assumptions, or folk beliefs, that still dominate today around learning in multiple languages, everyone who worked with him— even me—felt that he did not have the capacity to learn in multiple languages and somehow this negatively affected his linguistic and cognitive development. As the year progressed, and after several conferences, I suggested to the mother that he should learn only one language—he should only learn English.

Afterwards, my declaration bothered me. I said something that I rejected in my own home by raising my daughter to be bilingual and biliterate. Later, I came to the conclusion that my responses to bilingualism actually depended on how I foregrounded particular roles, either the "teacher role" or my "parent role." It was acceptable for me to raise my daughter bilingual, but with a child who did not fit into the mold of an "expected" student, language became the scapegoat for complex happenings that I could not explain.

I had a certain degree of power in the classroom to construct who this child could be because I was the teacher. It was assumed that I possessed some degree of knowledge about how to best educate children. Yet I realized that my actions could not only change experiences around language. They could also change families—families like my own—by perpetuating inequality among my students. I frequently asked myself, "Who am I to make major decisions about what language to speak in the homes of my students?" Remember that this boy's father could only speak Japanese. What would have happened to their relationship if they had followed through with my request?

Over the years of watching Emma, and later Ricky, and reflecting upon my teaching experiences and on Emma's early biliteracy through the data that I collected over four years, I realized that I initially defined biliteracy as a state in which two languages or written forms intermingle. In my quest for answers to questions that I raised about bilingual and biliterate children, I focused on how young children, such as the young child in my class, dealt with them as separate systems. Were there positive influences of languages intermingling, or could serious consequences arise? In fact, Wei argues that the word "bilingual" alone generally takes on the definition of someone in "possession of two languages" (2000: 7). What Emma showed me is that biliteracy is a way of life, a way of becoming someone within a cacophony of voices, ideologies, and identities that are encountered everyday in and out of the home. In addition, I acknowledged that instead of positioning different languages as separate systems, they needed to be seen as an overarching way of meaningful communication. In other words, literacy is built on theories of language, which have also engulfed the growing area of biliteracy. This requires asking essential questions around the meaning of language and its role in human existence.

And yet, mandated curricula leave little room to explore those questions. I have worked with teachers who teach in very diverse classrooms where they have as many as seven different language varieties. Working with them in classrooms, I came to the realization that although they work in the best interests of children, they carry with them folk beliefs around learning in multiple languages without truly understanding the different facets and the cognitive, social, and emotional benefits of early biliteracy—similar to me. Instead of thinking in terms of critical theory and literacy, they express frustration at the prescriptive literacy models pushed into their classrooms in which "good teaching" is compatible to dictating scripts. Standards, assessments, and policies governing how language should be used in the classroom with narrow focuses on phonemic awareness, phonics, fluency, vocabulary, and comprehension have filtered into classrooms and the hands of early biliterate children under the assumption that they will learn English as quickly and effectively as possible. These types of practices exert, at best, control over language and literacy. Where is the room for other languages? Where is the room for the rights of children around literacy? While this book only skims the surface of the daunting task of pushing out top-down learning models, it is my hope that it will continue the conversation by providing a space for the exploration and discussion of language rights.

Overview of the Book

The Introduction, Chapter 1, discusses a new way of thinking about biliteracy. Chapter 2 introduces Emma as a young child and the social context of the home. Chapters 3 addresses the complexity of writing across writing systems and provides a theoretical foundation for the work presented in this book. Chapter 4 examines the writing and drawing forms that result from Emma's active discovery when she was allowed to explore written forms of English and Japanese, while Chapter 5 situates written language as a cultural tool to raise the larger connection between writing and identity. The issue of identity will continue in Chapter 6, which addresses the relationships between learning to reading and identity through a code-switching lens. Chapter 7 describes what happened when Emma met the English-dominant world of school. Chapter 8 concludes the book with a summary discussion of the journey of becoming biliterate.

It is my hope that all of the chapters combined will provide unique perspectives that will further our thinking about the processes and the benefits of children becoming Biliterate/biliterate.

Acknowledgments

I would like to thank Emma for sharing her life with me. It is not always easy having a mother who is also an academic and a researcher, and Emma always took my audio and video recordings and my note-taking in good humor. Emma's excitement about me telling her story inspired me even more to make her voice heard in a time when silenced voices are privileged voices. To my son Rick, Jay, my sister Carrie, my mom Carol, and my dad John, they are the most supportive family anyone would be lucky to have. Without their patience and encouragement, my academic pursuits would never have been possible.

I am indebted to my mentors, friends, and fellow parent-researchers Denny Taylor and Marcia Baghban for reading through various stages of my manuscript. They continually pushed my thinking and were relentless in their belief in me and that this book has something to offer teachers and scholars. Most importantly, they taught me how to be my own person in my research and writing. I would like to thank Myra Zarnowski for her ongoing support. She always lent an ear for listening when I needed someone to share ideas, and was never shy about knocking on my door to ask for updates on the manuscript's progress.

I am sincerely grateful for my editor Naomi Silverman who gave me the chance to write this book.

CHAPTER 1

Introduction

A New Way of Thinking about Biliteracy

Becoming biliterate requires a deep understanding of human thought and the nature of language, both of which are increasingly narrowed within popular movements in education that attempt to locate language and reading difficulties in the human brain or to teach words detached from the emotional and experiential nature in which they find their meaning. Language, one of the most complex and abstract terms used by researchers, scholars, teachers, and lawmakers, is on the cusps of being trivialized to the point where the profound connections between us as human beings and our magnificent capacity to think, act, and react through language will be lost.

Recent advertisements for computer software programs claim that we can acquire a new language in the same ways that we learned our first language. The underlying premise behind this claim is that language is innate; all humans have the capacity to learn language in the form of oral sounds and grammatical structures through exposure (Chomsky, 2006). These two basic principles are founded on the psychological concepts that language is connected to the human brain, which holds an unlimited ability to process and produce a variety of language forms, whether through generating a variety of syntactical possibilities within a limited amount of grammatical structures (Chomsky, 2006) or through patterned stages in oral language development (Piaget & Inhelder, 2000). Many of these arguments have toppled over into the area of bilingualism in a cry to better understand the bilingual brain and its capacity to learn two languages.

Second Language Acquisition (SLA) theory evolved in response to much of the original research in bilingualism that suggested that the brain could not handle more than one language (Cummins, 1984; Krashen, 1982). Many bilingual behaviors, such as code switching, were used to defend the position that bilinguals were confused; they often interchanged languages or supplemented one language with words from another because they could not fully express themselves (Hakuta, 1986). However, SLA theory challenged these positions to propose that learning two languages at a young age results in advantages for children. Young children become more metacognitive with respect to language in general. Bilingual children were able to explain the English grammatical system and translate between multiple languages (Reyes, 2004). In essence, they developed an awareness that English is not the only language in the world. This ability gave children not only a linguistic advantage but also a social advantage over other monolingual children (Perez, 2004).

Language as a Symbol System

Language, however, is more than oral sounds and grammatical structures; it is a rich symbol system embodied with meaning, thoughts, and emotions. The research of Gardner (1982) and John-Steiner (1985) argue that there are different languages. While verbal language is one of them and bodily language evokes one of the earliest forms of thought, visual language and what John-Steiner (1985) calls "languages of emotion," or music, are also taken up by children to develop sensory experiences that ties words to human feelings.

Embodied Language

Piaget (1959; Piaget & Inhelder, 2000) contends that "knowledge is tied to actions" and children use their bodies as communication in their pre-verbal stages. Sometimes to the uneasy eyes of adults, children pick things up, squirm, throw objects, and take pens and mark the walls. John-Steiner (1985) argues that these "enactive representations" are a means for children to use their bodies to search out information about the meaning of things around them; they use their actions in the attempt to transform things in their environment. They learn cause—effect relationships, the physical build of objects, and object permanence (Piaget, 1959), just to name a few ideas, through their physical enactments in their environments.

Tools, which can take form of physical tools such as scissors, crayons, paper, stickers, and stationery along with other materials, play an important role in transformative actions (Kress, 1997; Rogoff, 2003; Vygotsky, 1986). Kress (1997) contends that children select particular physical tools based on "what is at hand," meaning that children will use what is available in their cultural settings. Engagement with tools is intertwined with developed thought (Wilson, 1998); children involve tools in problem-solving situations as they learn the expressive capacity that tools hold in developing effective communication.

There are, however, another set of tools that need to be distinguished from physical tools, and they are cultural tools. Cultural tools are specific to what culture provides. Verbal and written language forms are examples of cultural tools. While my family afforded my children with English and Japanese forms, both oral and written, as cultural tools, another household may present English, while another may have Arabic or Hebrew. Despite the fact that these households may supply similar physical tools to their children, such as scissors or crayons, the availability of different cultural tools in the forms of verbal and written languages shapes children's experiences as readers and writers. This idea that the forms of verbal and written languages play the role of cultural tools ties into how the social nature of texts are represented through cultural symbols (Holquist, 1981; Vygotsky, 1986). Oral and written forms of language provide the surface feature to language, and beneath that surface feature there are other qualities that provide a deeper meaning not always accessible to those outside the individual.

Language/language and Biliteracy/biliteracy

A distinction that differentiates the oral and written forms of language with its overall social and cultural meanings is required in order to appreciate the extent of becoming biliterate. On the one hand, English and Japanese are separate languages, with the little "l." They have different oral forms and internal structures. If someone does not have control of these surface forms, then that person may have problems with deriving meaning from what someone has said or written. And yet, at the same time, English and Japanese are not separate languages with the big "L."

Language (with the big "L") is more complex; it is tied to identity, emotion, and ways of thinking, believing, and acting. It is abstract and can only be inferred through how one uses the written and oral languages. Talking about the physical or verbal forms of Japanese and English only raises an awareness of the cultural tools that one has to work with, employ, or resource to re-enact identities, emotions, and belief systems. Because biliteracy is built on theories of language, biliteracy (with the little "b") involves the written forms and internal structures of languages and how they transact with one another. Biliteracy (with the big "B") holds more complex ties to who we are in a complex world of different languages (with the little "l").

In the past 20 years, we have come to learn more about the social and cultural nature of Language. Research has highlighted (1) how social and cultural driving forces give language meaning (Barton & Tusting, 2005; Gutierrez & Rogoff, 2003), (2) the interconnections between social and cultural identities and languages and how individuals redefine themselves through languages (Lave & Wenger, 1991; Toohey, 2000; Wenger, 1998), and (3) the social structures that reproduce and privilege particular forms and uses of languages (Auerbach, 1993; Collins, 1998; Tollefson, 1991). And yet, the more we learn about its uncontrollable nature, the more that we want to control it and package it into tidy stones. We test it; we dissect it. We try to teach and assess the minimal parts in order to cut the connections it offers to social and cultural domains and identities that give meaning to who we are.

A new way of thinking about biliteracy is needed to encompass the notion that becoming Biliterate (with the big "B") is first and foremost learning to become someone in this world. Emma has shown me this point through the many writings and snippets of dialogue that I have captured through the seven years of documenting her early biliteracy. These artifacts are akin to what John-Steiner (1985) calls "notebooks of the mind." Studying artists', writers', and composers' creative thought, John-Steiner argues that their notebooks represent "self-knowledge" or "intellectual labor" that is a "powerful resource for the understanding of thinking" and the "hidden processes of the mind" (1985: 1). Similar to these notebooks, Emma's artifacts left impressions that allowed me to explore the ways she used different languages to learn to be someone in this world. What I present in this book are my impressions of Emma, as well as the impressions that Emma left through her writings and dialogue, in order to better understand how she achieved what she needed to achieve to become Biliterate.

While I will use the general term biliteracy (with the little "b") throughout this book in discussing Emma's learning to read and write in English and Japanese, I reserve some space to come back to the term "Biliteracy" at the end of the book to rethink it as a right. In the end, this book is much more than learning to accommodate the oral and written forms of English and Japanese in learning to read and write. And for this reason, the reader will not find much reference to SLA or linguistic theories in learning two languages. I am not necessarily interested in whether Emma's biliteracy created "one language system" or "separate systems" (Genesee, 2000) for the reasons that I mentioned earlier. At the same time, terms can limit how ideas are framed.

Instead, this book is about the complexity to which Emma became *biliterate* as she navigated four written language forms in reading and writing and became *Biliterate* in order to actively define her sense of self, to gain access in the social and cultural spaces around her and to support her social, cognitive, and emotional well-being. At the same time, this book brings in schools and curricula.

There are many challenges that teachers and teacher-educators face today. We face political control, high stakes testing, and top-down curriculum models, and we also face challenges in how we can critically think about our own beliefs and teaching in the classroom. Testing and curricula are negatively changing the ways in which we teach children. Discourses are shifting and identities are being tied to labels such as "reader," "above grade level," and "below grade level." The discussion is not new, but the social and political realities in which these labels are occurring is menacing.

In this book, I hope to help recapture the space where there is room for critical thought and pedagogy around languages and literacies. For the very premise of this book lies on the notions that languages, both written and spoken, play substantive roles in learning and identity and that there are very crucial connections between critical teaching, critical teachers, and learning in multiple languages.

Summary

Teachers are bridges between their students and the dominant society. As I did, teachers can make decisions that can realign values around language and, in turn, families. However, my personal experiences suggest that through critical encounters with theory and practice, basic beliefs and assumptions can be transformed. Teachers are critical agents in challenging dominant beliefs to develop classroom practices for equity and social justice, and classrooms can be culturally responsive spaces where literacy learning in multiple languages takes place.

Teaching is a journey. We navigate through the unknown, we revel in our success, and sometimes wallow in our struggles. But it is always a journey of reinventing ourselves as individuals and teachers and a way to reconcile differences of perspectives, opinions, and beliefs about how and what children learn with how and what we should teach. In this book, I would like to take this journey together by introducing Emma, the person who encouraged me to rethink both by theoretical and pedagogical orientations toward literacy in multiple languages.

Emma's Biliteracy Timeline: 3 to 7 Years Old

The developmental history of written language, however, poses enormous difficulties for research. As far as we can judge from the available material, it does not follow a single direct line in which something like a clear continuity of forms is maintained. Instead, it offers the most unexpected metamorphoses, that is, transformations of particular forms of written language into others. Its line of development seems to disappear altogether; then suddenly, as if from nowhere, a new line begins, and at first it seems that there is absolutely no continuity between the old and the new. But only a naive view of development as a purely evolutionary process involving nothing but the gradual accumulation of small changes and the gradual conversion of one form into another can conceal from us the true nature of these processes

(Vygotsky, 1986: 106).

Emma's Biliteracy Timeline

2		
Years		Living in Japan and attending Japanese daycare
1 mo	First collected sample of Emma's writing: Lines and colors: red, yellow, white, light green, and dark green	
11 mo	First collected sample of a face (eyes, nose, mouth, cheeks, ears, and hair), circles, connected lines and circles, circles and lines to represent words. Appearance of the letter E	Moved to New York; Emma attends Little Gym; Emma's grandmother sends her books and "stuff" from Japan
3		
Years		Emma's first birthday party and begins attending other birthday parties, begins nursery school, ballet, and Japanese playgroups, and Japanese school
1 mo	First collected sample of B, D, R, borders. First cut-out sample	
2 mo	First collected sample of O, U, E, A (Figure 4.6), rainbows, Emma's name, facial expressions. String of letters to represent a word. Writes T-O's (Figure 4.10)	
3 mo	First collected sample of H, M, F, R, K, I, S; words, mommy and Rika; pictures, balloons, fruits, and apples. Writes P's with "a circle and a line" (Figure 4.5)	
4 mo	First collected sample of L, U, H; letter format and folded card; Emma's name in linear order	
5 mo	Invented scripts using attributes of the Roman alphabet and Japanese *hiragana* (Figure 4.3). Writes circular forms and read it as "Dear Mommy" (Figure 4.4)	Really into Disney Princesses and movies, as well as Japanese videos
6 mo	First collected sample of the name Sara written vertically (Figure 4.11). Wrote the *kanji* for rain (Figure 2.1)	
7 mo	First collected sample of G, W, B; alphabet; Daddy, get well, peace; Sentences, "I love Rika."; Get well card; cut-out hearts; drawings, hearts and flowers	
8 mo	Writes Mommy, Rika, and Emma and drew balloon in preschool (Figure 4.8)	
9 mo		
10 mo		
11 mo		
4		
Years		Begins 4-year-old class, begins Japanese kindergarten, stops Japanese playgroups, still receives books and packages from Japan. Becomes interested in computer games and software, begins violin lessons
1 mo	First ABC book. First collected samples of words: to, from, Julianne, and poetry forms.	
2 mo		
3 mo	First collected sample of Emma's full name in Japanese (Figures 4.9 and 5.2), words in Japanese *hiragana* (Figures 4.12 and 5.5)	
4 mo	Writes more Japanese friends' names in *hiragana*	
5 mo	First collected sample of a letter written to Emma in Japanese. Appearance of Rick's name	

(continued)

Age	Event	Milestone
6 mo		Ricky is born
7 mo		
8 mo		
9 mo	Draws environmental print in Japanese. Creates an origami book (Figure 5.8)	
10 mo		Becomes interested in Barbie, Dad begins watching baseball on TV
11 mo		
5 Years	Creates a baseball sign for Hideki Matsui (Figure 5.11)	Starts elementary school
1 mo	Attempts to copy sentences, homework, and "cursive" letters in Emma's name. Reads *Silly Sally* (Wood, 1994)	
2 mo	First collected sample of *katakana*. "Forgets" how to write her name	Kindergarten, starts piano and gymnastics
3 mo	Uses invented spelling to author a story book. Emma said "I don't want to be Japanese anymore."	
4 mo	Begins writing her name in Japanese on her school work	
5 mo	Writes in *hiragana* for an English-speaking family friend (Figure 5.1) Asks to go back to Japan. Emma asks, "If I was born in the Year of the Tiger, why do I speak English?"	
6 mo		
7 mo	Writes a birthday card for her friend using *hiragana* (Figure 5.12)	
8 mo		
9 mo	Reads *Otsukli Sama Konbawa* (Hayashi, 1986)	
10 mo	We visit Japan. Draws American and Japanese flags. Reads *Ushiro ni Iru no Dare* (Fukada, 2004). Reads *Kasa* (Matsuno, 1985)	
11 mo		
6 Years		Emma starts First Grade
1 mo		
2 mo	Writes a letter to her first grade teacher. Draws heart flowers and balloons. Reads *I Went Walking* (Williams, 1989)	
3 mo	Writes a "Roses are Red" poem. Writes sentences in school with sight words (Figure 7.1)	
4 mo		Takes karate classes Starts calligraphy in Japanese school
5 mo	Writes a Christmas list. Reads *Dear Zoo* (Campbell, 1982). Completes Japanese word plays in *Shimajiro* (Benesse, 2005). Writes school-based in the home (Figures 7.2 and 7.3)	
6 mo	Plays school and writes math worksheets. Reads Japanese word mazes with her father	
7 mo		
8 mo		
9 mo	Takes a survey of her friends. Creates a weather chart	
10 mo	Keeps a journal for Japanese school about growing a sunflower. Creates a "storybook" for Jay and my anniversary	
11 mo		
7 Years		

FROM EM MARIJUAN

CHAPTER 2

Emma as a Young Child

From the time Emma was born, she was socialized into ways of using Japanese and English in the home. Although we tried to divide the language use in the home (I spoke English while Jay spoke in Japanese), these permeable language boundaries were often crossed by the immediate family. For instance, I read both English and Japanese books to Emma. Her favorite English book was *Elmer Blunt's open house* (Novak, 1996), which I read repeatedly over the course of the two years that spanned our time in New York. At the same time, I also read Japanese storybooks that were mostly given to her by her grandparents. *Otsukisama konbawa* (*Good evening, Mr. Moon*) (Hayashi, 1986a) was a favorite of hers and triggered her to start pointing to the moon and saying, "Konbawa," or "Good evening."

These types of interactions illustrate how Emma's learning did not exist in isolation of outside social and cultural influences that shape the way that she learned. As researchers suggest, Emma's learning, as with all children, is inherently a social process. A sociocultural perspective on learning highlights children's construction of knowledge about written language by engaging in social activities with others. Emma wrote cards to her family and read the outside of cookie boxes, which often triggered a response from her father or me. Therefore, instead of asking how reading and writing development emerge, we should ask how social and cultural practices give rise to children's participation in reading and writing activities (Gee, 2002). This shift in focus encourages us to view Emma's learning through the lens of how her home and community created social structures for

Emma to interact with different types of reading and writing practices around English and Japanese (Taylor, 1983).

By participating in activities around language, Emma learned through English and Japanese and learned about them. Language became the medium through which relationships with family members developed and changed. As we actively engaged Emma in reading and writing activities, she could take on different roles and participate in social and cultural activities in the home (Rogoff, 2003). Emma may have been a listener in one context, but in another she may have attempted to recreate language for her own purposes based on what she has already experienced.

In addition, languages were not used equivalently in the home. Naturally, living in Japan allowed for more Japanese than English immersion. Listening to Japanese on television, observing Japanese print in the environment, and attending Japanese day care created a Japanese-dominant social context within which Emma was an active participant. Yet, by the time Emma was 2 years old, she spoke in one-word utterances from both languages, such as saying "dame" for "no," and "water" for "mizu." By the time Emma was 2 years, 5 months old, we were already living in New York and she was talking in more complex sentence structures in both languages (such as "Iku yo" and "Let's go"). However, Emma did not always align her conversation with the language preferences of the people whom she was addressing. Although her Japanese grandmother does not speak English, Emma would tell her, "Let's go" when she wanted to go outside in our garden.

Multiple Social Practices

Emma participated in a variety of social practices that invoked both languages inside and outside of the home. Social practices frame the ways in which we engage with others. Children play with friends; they may go to preschool or gym classes. Each of these practices has particular ways of using both oral and written language. Our move to New York heralded a switch in culture, social activities, and language use. Naturally, the Japanese-dominant community was replaced by an English-speaking environment. Yet Jay and I tried to keep our language use consistent with the bilingual atmosphere that we created in Japan in the home. Developing a linguistically diverse atmosphere allowed Emma to learn multiple written languages by becoming an active member in her home and community (Gregory et al., 2004). In many ways, as I will illustrate throughout this book, Emma did not see her participation in different linguistic communities as separate but, instead, her engagement with language and others as permeating linguistic boundaries allowing her to live within "simultaneous worlds" (Gregory et al., 2004; Kenner, 2004). Consequently, the nature of the social practices in which Emma participated was fluid and evolving as she grew older and her interests changed and as she attempted to develop relationships with others in her immediate environment. Some of the major social practices that were influential in her everyday life include:

- **Mommy and Me classes.** Emma and I attended Mommy and Me classes two days a week. One class was for Japanese families and was run by a woman in our neighborhood. The other class was a gym class from a corporate, chain gym company.
- **Play dates.** Emma had regular play dates with both Japanese- and English-speaking children. I became friends with other Japanese wives who had also moved from Japan to New York, and our children became friends. We set up regular and rotating play dates for our children. Additionally, Emma had play dates with English-speaking friends from her Mommy and Me classes and her preschool classes.
- **Birthday parties.** Birthday parties were a commonly occurring social event for Emma. She attended a variety of types of parties which included gym parties, dress-up parties, and cooking parties.
- **Holidays.** Holidays such as Halloween, Christmas, and Easter influenced the types of activities in which Emma participated within a calendar year. For example, when she went to see Santa, she wanted to write a letter, or when it was time for Halloween, she drew Halloween pictures and taped them on her bedroom door.
- **Preschool.** Emma attended a local preschool for three hours a day starting at age 3. Emma's class was an English-dominant class; however, she had one Japanese-speaking friend named Keisuke in her 3-year-old class, who she knew before she entered preschool. On the other hand, her 4-year-old class consisted of all English-dominant children.
- **Japanese school.** Emma attended a weekly Japanese school at age 3 at the same time that she entered a two-hour preschool class. She attended the preschool class for one year and then progressed to a Japanese kindergarten class. Japanese kindergarten starts from age 4 and lasts for two years; thus, Emma continued in kindergarten until age 6.
- **Familial practices in the home.** This category covers a wide and general range of regular activities in the home and consisted of activities performed using both languages. Emma watched English and Japanese videos, read books written in both languages, and played English and Japanese games. Emma also enjoyed completing Japanese

activity books called *Shimajiro* with her father, which will be elaborated on in the following section. This category also includes American popular-culture activities for children, such as playing Barbies and collecting Disney princesses.

The social practices that shaped Emma's experiences were rich, varied, and dynamic in their language and literacy uses, and were—importantly—highly complex. Although I have tried to categorize them here as separate entities for discussion's sake, the boundaries between the social practices were fluid. Activities in the home were influenced by holidays and play dates that Emma was having. In turn, her language use may have been tied not only to social practices but also to who the participants were in the immediate context. For instance, she often spoke with Keisuke in Japanese in English-speaking preschool because he was Japanese-dominant. Therefore, building social relationships influenced language use within a variety of contexts and Emma did not necessarily see language learning as language separation, in which she needed to separate languages depending on context. Instead, Emma appeared to draw on a variety of linguistic resources to communicate and construct meaning.

Activity Books

An example of drawing on available linguistic resources during Emma's engagement in activities is illustrated in Emma's love of completing Japanese activity books with her father. These Japanese activity books were sent by her Japanese grandmother. After moving to New York, Emma's grandmother was concerned that Emma would not be able to communicate in Japanese. In order to encourage Emma to maintain ties to Japanese language and culture, Emma's grandmother sent books every month, and Emma enjoyed completing these books with her father. They would work together reading, writing, cutting, and gluing activities from the book.

Emma's favorite was *Shimajiro*, an activity book that featured a little tiger named Shimajiro and his family, and we will see different reading and writing samples that evolved out of Emma's interactions with *Shimajiro*. The nature of the book required adult participation for reading directions and cutting and tearing out objects that were included in the book. Furthermore, *Shimajiro* consisted of monthly themed issues that centered mostly on family, seasons, holidays, animals, friends, and manners. As the age-level progressed, themed issues that addressed the Japanese writing system and numbers were also included in each book. Additional resources such as charts, games, puppets, and manipulative items supplemented the major content of the theme. While Japanese activity books were used as a teaching tool in the home, they also created a space in which Emma and her father could build and develop relationships with each other. In this way, Emma did not just learn about the content presented in each book, she also learned something about herself.

In one particular interaction with Jay, Emma was trying to locate cities on a map of Japan. Once she found the city, Emma needed to put a sticker on its location.

"Where's Tokyo?" Emma asked her father.

"Tokyo desyo [Tokyo is here]," Jay replied. "Sore kara. Itta onsen wa kono hen da yo." Jay immediately added that the hot spring bath that we went to during our last trip to Japan was located nearby Tokyo.

"Koko?" Emma asked if it was here.

"Ishikawa-ken." Jay responded that where Emma was pointing was Ishikawa Prefecture.

Emma was still a little unsure and replied, "I don't know. I'll put the sticker . . ." Emma code switched to here in Japanese, "koko."

This dialogue illustrates how the home supported a blending of language forms. The written text was Japanese while the spoken text was in English and Japanese. At the same time, we can see evidence of how Jay guided Emma's participation to reach the goal of the activity; he was trying to move her forward in her learning. During this process, Jay accepted Emma's code switching and recognized it as purposeful. While I cannot deny that Emma is learning something about the geography of Japan, I suggest that she is also learning something about herself by actively using language and observing other people's reactions to her language use in her everyday life.

Early Writing and Drawing

Emma's earliest attempts at writing and drawing were a means of organizing ideas into different forms and making sense of her experiences. Table 2.1 outlines the number of writing and drawing samples that were collected between the ages of 3 and 7 years. These samples were categorized

Table 2.1 Emma's self-produced writing and drawing samples collected between 3 and 7 years.

	Age							
Languages	3–4 years		4–5 years		5–6 years		6–7 years	
English	76	56.7%	30	36.6%	37	58.7%	70	88.2%
Japanese	0	0	20	24.4%	20	31.7%	3	3.2%
Both	1	0.7%	3	3.7%	3	4.8%	0	0
Image only	57	42.5%	29	35.4%	3	4.8%	20	21.5%
Total	134		82		63		93	

as self-produced, meaning that Emma created them herself on blank paper. The table is broken down into four main categories: writing in English, writing in Japanese, writing in both English and Japanese, and drawing only images. Samples that included both writing and drawing were counted toward the writing categories.

Emma enjoyed making signs from a young age and was motivated and searched out other people as models and guides for her writing. Writing, consequently, was not an individual undertaking; instead, it was a social act resulting in Emma writing with other people. Viewing family members as "experienced" in the skills of written language, she often asked her father, aunt, or me to write her name or to draw pictures. Observing our efforts and attempting to approximate what we did in our writing was one way in which Emma's writing began to take more conventional forms. Emma drew pictures of friends, family, and objects in her environment; she created birthday cards and signs that she would tape to the walls or doors. Emma's biliteracy timeline that precedes this chapter provides added details to Table 2.1 by helping to highlight Emma's diverse drawing and writing abilities and to summarize the content and sequence of the writing and drawing samples that will be presented in this book.

Using a biliteracy timeline allows us to document the different forms that appeared in Emma's signs and the different functions that writing and drawing served for her. At the same time, the social practices that Emma participated in are also documented because these experiences influenced the particular forms that her signs took. When Emma went to a birthday party, she wanted to draw a picture of her friend as a "card"; from reading books with family members, she learned that she could arrange her folded origami animals into a book. Everyday social practices, such as going to school, playing with friends, and attending birthday parties coordinated her life. Not only did Emma learn about how life was categorized into routines through language from participating in these social events, she also learned that there are written objects associated with these routines; environmental print, books, magazines, and notes written on paper mediated the ways that she participated in activity. Here I will highlight some of the dominant themes that arose and are highlighted on her biliteracy timeline.

Early Writing in English

Overlapping, colored lines were the first forms that her signs took (see timeline). These types of controlled marks preceded any type of labeling, meaning that Emma did not necessarily view her marks as a specific object. Many would agree that these forms are more related to drawing than writing because children's attempts at writing with lines are smaller and more controlled (Harste et al., 1984). As the timeline illustrates, Emma was writing in English before Japanese. In fact, as Table 2.1 shows, 56.7% of the artifacts collected between 3 and 4 years of age were written in English, and 41% of her artifacts involving drawing. During this age span, there was one sample that possessed both English and Japanese. The first letters to appear in her writing were those of her name and letters. Other letters such as "O," "U," "B," "D," and "R" quickly followed. While some of her beginning English writing involved strings of letters that she would read as a word (first appeared at 3 years, 2 months), other writing samples consisted of letters that were spread out over the page. At the same time, between the ages of 3 and 4, Emma went from writing strings of letters to writing close to conventional sentences. At 3 years, 7 months, Emma wrote a get-well card on which the sentence "I lb Rika" ("I love Rika") appeared.

However, between 4 and 5 years of age, English decreased to 36.6% while Japanese increased to 24.4%, but English increased again to 58.7% when Emma entered kindergarten at 5 years. By this time, Emma's English writing became more sophisticated. She was writing lists, exploring with font by writing in bubble letters and cursive, and creating storybooks. Furthermore, there was a drastic increase in English between the ages of 6 and 7 when Emma was in First Grade. Unlike in the previous year, this increase in English resulted in a significant decrease in Japanese in the home.

Writing in Japanese

Written Japanese, which has four scripts: *hiragana, katakana, kanji* (or Chinese characters), and the Roman alphabet (and will be described in further detail in Chapter 3), appeared when Emma was 3 years, 6 months. Emma was in my bedroom watching a morning cartoon. On the floor with a black marker and a small stack of white paper, she wrote a string of letters and then the *kanji* for rain (see Figure 2.1). Holding up her paper, she said, "Mommy, look. I made the *kanji* for rain." Afterwards, I asked if she would like to write the *kanji* for our last name, "Kabuto." I modeled it for her on the paper, and she attempted it on her own. This initial sample included both Japanese and English, which I mentioned earlier was the sole sample that included a Japanese script that I collected between the ages of 3 and 4.

However, Japanese increased between 4 and 5 years of age to 24.4%. *Hiragana*, or the cursive form of Japanese characters, appeared at 4 years, 3 months. This increase was related to the *Shimajiro* books that Emma received. Using the books as a model for writing in *hiragana*, Emma began seeing the possibilities of using Japanese. While the year before she was

MARCH 2002

Figure 2.1 Emma (3 years, 6 months) wrote her name and the *kanji* for rain, *ame*.

Source: Taylor et al. 2002. © 2002 by the National Council of Teachers of English. Used with permission.

writing her Japanese friends' names in English (such as Rika), she now wrote them in *hiragana*.

There was another increase in Japanese between 5 and 6 years of age to 31.7%. During this time span, the use of both English and Japanese increased due to the fact that Emma created fewer drawing samples. The amount of drawing samples that I collected dropped from 35.4% between 4 and 5 years to 4.8% between 5 and 6 years. By the end of First Grade, Japanese writing declined, and only 3.2% of the samples that I collected in the home consisted of writing in Japanese. This decline does not mean that Emma no longer wrote in Japanese. Emma was still attending Japanese school and wrote Japanese in school and on homework. And yet, in spite of the fact that Emma was writing in each language within its respective schooling context and the continual presence of both languages in the home, there were shifts in her self-produced writing to English by the end of Emma's first-grade year.

Writing in English and Japanese

Emma did not always separate or isolate English and Japanese. As researchers would suggest, they worked together to create meanings within her signs (Kenner & Kress, 2003). Viewing each script as an organized way of constructing meaning, Emma's use of script switching was meaningful and purposeful (Kenner & Kress, 2003), and a small percentage of her writing samples from 3 to 6 years of age incorporated both scripts. An early example of this is Emma's envelope addressed to her friend Keisuke (Emma was 5 years, 6 months old; see timeline). For Christmas, Emma received a badge-making kit. She decided to make a badge for each one of her friends. Instead of wrapping it, she placed the badge inside of an envelope and wrote "From Emma, to . . ." on a white strip of paper, which she stapled to the envelope. Although she gave most of them away, there were some left in the house, one of which was Keisuke's. Emma and Keisuke played together and were in both the same preschool and Japanese Saturday school; they spoke in both languages and often code switched. Emma's crafting of Keisuke's card in many ways mirrored the social and language relationships that she held with him. They lived in simultaneous language and sociocultural communities, and Emma's card needed to represent that fact, which she did by writing in multiple languages. Script-switching samples remained at a relatively low percentage: 0.7% between 3 and 4 years; 3.7% between 4 and 5 years; 4.8% between 5 and 6 years; and 0% between 6 and 7 years. While this may be the case, as I will describe later in Chapter 5, script-switching samples provide significant insights into the intersection of English and Japanese and the roles they played in defining Emma's sense of self.

Creating Images

Images were another mode in Emma's signs. Emma's earliest artifacts which were created prior to age 4 were composed mostly of images. She often drew self-portraits or pictures of her family. Drawings became the earliest forms of writing and labeling for Emma. Before she could write her name with letters, she drew pictures of herself. Her earliest images of people consisted of primary attributes related to shape and lines (Heath & Wolf, 2004). Emma drew large circles for the face and smaller circles for individual facial features (eyes, nose, and mouth), and lines represented the mouth. There were times when she labeled her pictures with names or asked a family member to label them for her. As Emma's drawing development progressed, she was able to attend to more individual attributes to distinguish objects. For instance, eyes became brown circles, and the mouth was a red line. This attention to detail was the result of Emma's looking and noticing of how objects can be differentiated. Image-only samples fluctuated from 3 to 7 years of age. While they appeared to decrease by age 6, there was another increase between 6 and 7 years. Overall, Emma valued the roles and purposes of both writing and drawing throughout her early childhood.

Images played decorative functions as well. Drawing hearts and flowers became a trademark of Emma's signs and became linked to her identity as a sign-maker. For instance, when she was 6 years old, instead of drawing a family tree, Emma created a family flower in which each petal represented a family member. The combination of images and writing show that Emma understood that each mode served functions in her overall meaning of what she wanted to create.

Examples of Language and Discourses within Emma's Early Writing

In the broadest sense, language is composed of discourses (Gee, 1996). For instance, when I teach in the college where I work, I tend to use academic discourses in my lectures. Someone who is not studying to be a teacher may come to my class in the middle of the semester and have a difficult time following my lectures because they have not been socialized into that particular type of discourse over the course of the semester. Yet when I am in my office I may receive a phone call from Emma and use a social, everyday discourse with her. These categories can be broken down even further. Academic discourses can be connected to other types of domains, such as those in the medical field and business fields. At the same time, social languages can also have multiple uses. Teenage friends and work colleagues use different types of social languages with each other.

Emma displayed different degrees of bilingualism depending on the type of discourse in which she engaged. When Emma was in her 4-year-old preschool Japanese school class, they studied the planets. While her social Japanese discourse appeared proficient, she had a difficult time with more complex and academic language expressions in Japanese, such as naming the planets. This was particularly true as her schooling in English increased. In spite of the fact that she attended Japanese school on Saturday, the number of hours in preschool and elementary school outnumbered those spent in Japanese school. Consequently, her flexibility in using a variety of discourses in English accelerated while her Japanese proficiencies began to slow.

Similarly, writing in two languages also required the knowledge of written discourses, both academic and social. While I have provided an overall pattern of written language use within Emma's early writing and drawing samples, there is more substance to the writing and drawing in how they involved different types of discourses. For instance, Emma's envelope to Keisuke used a particular type of genre. Using "from" and "to," Emma recognized that this type of wording signaled a particular type of activity. Her written discourse matched its social purpose, illustrating how language forms and social functions work together. In this case, she was using it with a Japanese-speaking friend. Again, proficiency in written discourses is fluid. While Emma tended to use "to" and "from" with all of her friends regardless of the languages they spoke before the age of 5, by the time she was 5 years, 6 months old she could use *he* and *kara* for the same social purposes. As a result, her written language usage evolved as she incorporated discourses related to Japanese.

The more experienced that Emma became as a writer, the more different types of discourses began to appear in her writing. The following provides a list of the different discourse that she used within her writing samples.

- **Letter-writing**. Emma wrote cards and letters to different people, particularly to her family and friends. She used letter language for her audience.
- **Signs**. Emma created signs that she posted around the house. In one particularly memorable sign, Emma drew a picture of her brother with a circle and slash through it and wrote, "Do Not Enter," which she posted on the door to our den.
- **Lists**. Emma wrote a variety of lists. In one example, she wrote a *Monday List*, on which she wrote, "Wake up. Go to school. Come home." Emma also drew boxes before each phrase, which she crossed off.
- **School**. Emma attempted to "play school" which involved using school-based discourses. She developed worksheets, tests, and homework for imaginary people and graded them.
- **Childhood pop culture**. Emma often included the names of pop-culture objects, items, dolls, or toys. For instance, Emma may have written "Shimajiro" or "Barbie" on a sheet of paper. The Disney princesses were Emma's favorite pop-culture items between the ages of 4 and 7. There were times when she drew pictures of them alongside herself or wrote their names on sheets of paper.

"I Don't Want to Be Japanese Anymore"

As I have portrayed, by the time Emma was 5 years, 3 months old, she was a beginning reader and writer in three Japanese writing forms and in English. She was speaking English and Japanese inside and outside the home, as well as participating in a variety of social practices and developing relationships with other people in her environment. However, one November evening before bed, Emma who was three months into kindergarten, asked her father to play sumo wrestling.

"Please, daddy. One time," Emma begged.

"Ashita [tomorrow]," her father replied.

Then Emma said, "Daddy, I don't want to be Japanese anymore."

"Soo [really]," her father said. "Zyaa, sumo shiyo," he continued by agreeing with Emma to play sumo.

Each took opposing stances and placed one fist on the ground to charge after the cue *take no okota* was given.

Emma's comment was a passing but critical moment. Why would an early proficient bilingual-biliterate child, who has a wealth of working knowledge about both Japanese and English, suggest to her father that she wanted to change part of her cultural, language, and national identities? Responses to this question are not as straightforward as one might expect. Two months later Emma asked me, "If I was born in the Year of the Tiger, why do I speak English?" In addition, three months later, she wrote her name on her English homework in Japanese next to her English name. When I asked her why she did so, she replied, "Because I'm the only one in my class who can speak Japanese, so no one will know what I am writing."

Emma's comments suggest that language is much more than written and oral forms, words, and discourses. Language also embodies identities that connect people to their social groups; it can align speakers with particular groups, while creating an otherness for those outside the group (Wei, 2000). Being able to control and demonstrate proficiency in multiple written languages and spoken discourses is not sufficient to define what it means to become biliterate. It also means being able to understand the multiple social and cultural spaces within which one participates; becoming biliterate also involves identity work.

Identity

Identity is a very complex concept to discuss. Depending on the field of study and discipline, definitions can range from identity as a fixed notion (e.g., being "a female" or "a male") to being socially constructed (Holland et al., 1998; Ivanic, 1988). While the former definition suggests that identity is immune to change and contestation, the latter proposes that people have agency in the process of shaping an identity. That is, they have the ability to change and evolve and can select from possibilities in their social environment to recreate who they are. At the same time, identities are multiple. We can have different types of "selves" that make up who we are: a teacher, a mother, a wife, and a friend are examples of different types of roles that we may play.

Language and literacy can be media in which people reproduce, challenge, or evolve their identities. By supporting a blending of language forms in the home, Jay and I helped to socially construct who Emma was as a biliterate child. If we had chosen to restrict our language use to either English or Japanese, Emma would have had different experiences in her developing biliteracy. In addition, she may have seen herself differently in relation to others around her.

Consequently, as Emma wrote in Japanese and English to a family member or a friend, she was reproducing a particular type of self and making connections with others through language, which was a cultural tool for Emma to employ as a way to mediate the relationships she created with others. There were also times when she tried to work through the dynamics within her identities through language. Emma's comment that she did not "want to be Japanese anymore" demonstrated the multiplicity in her identities; there were times when pieces of her identity competed with each other and created tension. An example from my experience involves my role as "mother" and as "researcher" in this work. When Emma said that she did not want to be Japanese anymore, my mother side felt shocked and hurt by her comment. Yet, in my researcher role, I saw this comment as important, and it eventually influenced the ways in which I examined Emma's early biliteracy. That is, I felt guilt, shock, and revelations all at the same time. Thus, we can have an otherness to our identities (Kristeva, 2003).

Consequently, Emma struggled with the multiple roles she had taken on in her life. However, her struggles were constantly in motion. When she wrote her name in Japanese on her English homework, she challenged the notion that she needed to have one or the other; she recognized that she could have multiple existences. At the same time, she recognized that this multiplicity in her identity allowed her access to and power in different social groups. So, while her name in English accessed power in an English-speaking environment such as her kindergarten classroom, writing in Japanese also gave a certain power—a way of saying "I'm special" because "I'm the only one who can read what I wrote." Learning to read and write in two languages was a way in which Emma was able to construct who she was as a bilingual and biliterate child and to work out the dynamics and tensions in her identity.

Summary

The linguistic aspects and the evolution of the forms of spoken and written languages are both important factors in learning to write in two languages. How one language influenced the other and how Emma made connections between English and Japanese were important to the process of becoming biliterate. However, should we consider Emma's perceptions of herself as a biliterate person? In addition, how does the degree of biliteracy play into the picture? If we did consider these questions, then perhaps Emma's perceptions of herself may redefine what it means for her to be bilingual and biliterate over time.

Speaking, reading, and writing in English and Japanese were acts, and they were not synonymous to but parts of bilingualism and biliteracy. Biliteracy is seen as social practices in which languages are cultural tools in learning, developing social relationships, and evolving language and social identities. Emma's bilingualism and biliteracy were not solely about learning phonemic sounds, writing conventional words, and reading accurately. They were, first and foremost, about sociocultural knowledge and learning to be who she is in this world. Taking this stance, the following chapters will delve deeper into Emma's experiences to examine her early biliteracy in order to paint a portrait of it as socially driven and comprising of complex, multidimensional acts.

Reaction Question

What would you do as a teacher if you heard Emma say that she did not want to be Japanese anymore?

Suggested Activities

1. Observe and document the biliteracy learning of young children. Collect observational and interview notes on the different social practices in which they participate. Also, collect writing and drawing artifacts and note the appearances and evolutions of how they use written language. Describe their experiences by creating a biliteracy timeline.
2. Conduct oral language histories on bilingual/biliterate individuals. Ask them to talk about their bilingualism and biliteracy. You can develop questions that focus on the following areas:
   • Do they consider themselves to be bilingual and biliterate?
   • How did they learn to be bilingual and biliterate?
   • When do they feel comfortable speaking in each language? Uncomfortable?

- When do they feel comfortable reading and writing in each language? Uncomfortable?

Analyze their responses for:

- the social driving forces that encouraged or discouraged learning in multiple languages;
- relationships between language and identity;
- the variety of social practices that supported learning in multiple languages;
- the advantages of bilingualism and biliteracy;
- the degree of proficiency depending on different discourses.

CHAPTER 3

Writing across Writing Systems

Theoretical Approaches

As I introduced in the previous chapter, although Emma was far from writing conventionally in either language by the time she was 5 years old, she demonstrated the developing ability and desire to write across scripts depending upon her interests and audience. As I observed Emma learning to navigate two very different writing systems, the question that constantly came to my mind was how did she do it? At such a young age, how did she learn the forms of four scripts: three in Japanese and one in English? But before I can engage in this discussion, I must first address the question of what makes a writing system.

What Makes a Writing System?

Writing is probably one of the most prized possessions of any civilization. In its most common sense, writing allows us to put speech into written forms to communicate ideas. We do so by understanding that there are particular components of writing that aid us in developing what we want to communicate. First, we need to understand that there are conventional written forms to writing. These written forms are related to cultures. While written forms can consist of spellings and punctuation, or orthographies, they are also related to writing directionality such as whether we write from left to right or right to left. Written language, at the same time, is associated with oral language which is made up of sounds, or phonology. While there are many characteristics that define writing systems, I will focus on three overall characteristics, which are written language forms, relationships between phonology and orthography, and internal structure.

Written Language Forms

Writing systems used around the world are classified based on what they represent: pictures or ideas, syllables, or individual sounds that make up syllables (Sassoon, 1995). Logo-syllabic writing systems, such as Chinese, are written forms which are a descendant of pictographs. Japanese, on the other hand, incorporates two syllabic systems—*hiragana* and *katakana*—in which each symbol represents a syllable. English is an example of an alphabetic system that use letters (or groups of letters) to represent individual sounds (or groups of sounds).

Writing in an Alphabetic System

English employs the Roman alphabet. The graphic forms that make up a writing system are called graphemes, and the modern Roman alphabet possesses 26 graphemes, or letters from "A" to "Z." In its current use, the modern version of the Roman alphabet evolved from the Latin one used by the Romans around the 1st century B.C. As with many other writing systems, the Latin alphabet was not invented by the Romans who instead modified the Greek alphabet that was brought over to Italy by Greek sailors around the 3rd century B.C.

Writing in an Logo-Syllabic System

The basis of a logo-syllabic system is the pictogram or a combination of pictograms. One of the earliest forms of writing, pictograms are simplified drawings used to represent objects. Pictograms have also been known to convey ideas, which are known as ideograms.

The Chinese writing system was developed about 2000 B.C. and systemized between 200 B.C. and A.D. 200. Chinese characters fall into three main categories: the pictogram, an abstract pictogram, and a semantic radical and a phonetic component (Rogers, 2005).

Certain Chinese characters evolved directly from a picture. An example of such a character is that of "lady, woman, or girl," 女 which was originally a picture of a woman before it took its current form. Abstract pictograms are characters that represent abstract ideas or concepts such as the characters for numbers shown in Figure 3.1. Although Chinese characters have a phonetic component, they are built with a strong semantic base, meaning that characters carry specific meanings. For instance, if the character for girl, 女 is combined with 王, meaning "king, rule or magnate," the combination 女王 becomes "woman king," or "queen."

More complex characters are made up of two parts—the semantic

一	二	三	四	五	六	七	八	九	十
1	2	3	4	5	6	7	8	9	10

Figure 3.1 Chinese characters for the numbers 1–10.

component and the phonetic component—that create one character. The semantic component is also called the "radical." The character for woman 女 can be a semantic component. Take for instance the character for daughter, 娘, which is a complex character. The character 女 is the left side radical and the right side of 娘 possesses the phonetic component that clues the reader into the character's pronunciation.

Each Chinese character is considered a grapheme (Rogers, 2005). When writing characters, the stroke order, or the order that the *kanji* is written in, is considered extremely important in creating visually accurate characters. While stroke orders can range from one to 30 per *kanji* and variations can occur, the general rule is that a character is written from left to right and from top to bottom, and horizontal lines are made before vertical ones.

Writing in a Syllabic System

The earliest form of a syllabic writing was cuneiform. Dating back to 1400–1200 B.C., cuneiform evolved from pictograms but was meant to be read phonetically. Known as one of the most complicated written languages, Japanese is an example of syllabic writing in the modern day. As a mixed writing system, Japanese incorporates Chinese characters, which are called *kanji* in Japanese, and two syllabic *kana* systems—*hiragana* and *katakana*, and the Roman alphabet.

There is little evidence to suggest that Japan had a writing system before borrowing Chinese characters roughly 1,700 years ago (Rogers, 2005). Scholars suggest that the Chinese writing system was brought to Japan by Koreans who traveled between China and Japan. There are other accounts of Japanese monks who traveled to China to study and brought the Chinese writing system back to Japan to educate the Japanese.

Chinese characters served as a starting point for graphemes for the Japanese language but also provided some difficulties as the Chinese and Japanese languages have different structures. For instance, Chinese is ordered like English in a subject–verb–object sequence. Japanese, contrarily, is ordered subject–object–verb. In addition, Chinese verbs are conjugated differently than Japanese verbs that have complex conjugations to show present, past, future, infinitives, and present-perfect forms.

Consequently, the Japanese developed two additional syllabic scripts, *hiragana* and *katakana* (see Figure 3.2). *Hiragana* and *katakana* are used

あ	い	う	え	お
ア	エ	ウ	エ	オ
A	I	U	E	O

か	き	く	け	こ
カ	キ	ク	ケ	コ
Ka	Ki	Ku	Ke	Ko

さ	し	す	せ	そ
サ	シ	ス	セ	ソ
Sa	Shi	Su	Se	So

た	ち	つ	て	と
タ	チ	ツ	テ	ト
Ta	Ti	Tu	Te	To

な	に	ぬ	ね	の
ナ	ニ	ヌ	ネ	ノ
Na	Ni	Nu	Ne	No

は	ひ	ふ	へ	ほ
ハ	ヒ	フ	へ	ホ
Ha	Hi	Hu	He	Ho

ま	み	む	め	も
マ	ミ	ム	め	モ
Ma	Mi	Mu	Me	Mo

や		ゆ		よ
Ya		Yu		Yo

ら	り	る	れ	ろ
ラ	リ	ル	レ	ロ
Ra	Ri	Ru	Re	Ro

わ				を
ワ				--
Wa				Wc

Figure 3.2 Three of the four graphemes used in writing Japanese. The top row of each set is written in *hiragana*, the second row in *katakana*, and the third row in the Romanization of syllabic graphemes.

to represent the same sounds but have different purposes in writing. *Hiragana* is known as the cursive formation and is employed in informal texts. Some of the purposes of *hiragana* are to indicate the pronunciation of unknown *kanji*, write first and given Japanese names, and teach Japanese children beginning writing. People write borrowed words from other languages in *katakana* (including foreign names) and for emphasizing particular words.

In addition to these three scripts, Romanization has become increasingly popular in Japan in the later 20th century. Romanization involves writing the Japanese phonology in the Roman alphabet, which will be the technique that I will use in subsequent chapters for Japanese spoken or written texts. In addition, certain borrowed words or abbreviations are written in the Roman alphabet. For instance, in Japanese, a lady who works in an office is called an "OL," which is short for "office lady." "OL" appears in this manner in written texts.

All four scripts are used simultaneously in Japanese. Below is a typical Japanese sentence that has three of the four scripts.

明日イエスリ‐ム一を買います

(Tomorrow) (ice cream) (will buy)

The sentence reads, "Tomorrow, I will buy ice cream." There are three scripts employed here. "Tomorrow" (明日) and root of the verb "buy" (買) are written in Chinese characters. "Ice cream" (イエスリ‐ム一) is a borrowed word, and, therefore, written in *katakana*. The verb suffix of "buy" (います) is written in *hiragana*.

Phonology and Orthography

The ability to read written languages is what gave birth to the notion of literacy. Historically, this capacity was held by an elite few such as monks, priests, scribes, or transcribers, who were regarded highly within society. But in modern society the ability to read is held by the masses rather than the few. Part of reading written marks is developing an awareness of the systematic organization of graphemes into spellings, or orthography, in relation to the system of sounds present within the respective oral language, or phonology. I emphasize *part of reading* because reading is first and foremost about understanding. Even with superior knowledge of the relationships between written marks and phonology, if there is a lack of comprehension of what we orally produce then there is little point of reading. While many researchers will not argue this point, they will argue the best route to take toward comprehension (Goodman, 1996; Shaywitz, 2003). Many of the contentions lie in the role of phonics, which are the relationships between phonology and a system of spellings. While some researchers believe that systematic phonics instruction will lead to automatic word recognition, which then will allow the reader to focus on comprehension (Adams, 1994; Shaywitz, 2003), others contend that readers select from a variety of reading cues, graphophonics, or the symbol and sound relationship, being one of them (Goodman, 1996; Smith, 1994). Through this body of research, we have come to understand just how inexact the English phonology–orthography relationship is because of English's lack of a pure one-to-one, letter-to-sound basis (Goodman, 1996). Since scholars in the field of education have illustrated how the phonology and orthography relationships have been influenced by factors other than the sounds of language (Strauss, 2005).

Alphabetic Languages

The alphabet allows for flexibility in representing sounds that logographic and syllabic writing systems do not. Using an alphabet requires a limited number of letters that have specialized sounds which are then combined to make words. For instance, the word "cat" has three phonemes, or the smallest units of sound. If we know that "C" is /c/, "A" is /a/, and "T" is /t/, then we can put them together to write the word "cat." This example illustrates a strong degree of correspondence between sounds and graphemes. But English has what linguists describe as a deep orthographic depth. Orthographic depth refers to the relationship between oral language and writing, and languages with deep depth have little one-to-one correspondence between oral sounds and written language (Rogers, 2005). Linguists argue that there are very complex relationships between phonology and orthography in English. Children's invented spellings illustrate many of these complications.

Take, for instance Figure 3.3 in which Emma (5 years, 8 months) wrote, "Me and my friends are playing dress up." Emma's kindergarten writing illustrates two major points of English orthography. First, phonemes are perceptual constructs, and we assign sound-graphic patterns to what we think we hear (Goodman, 1996; Strauss, 2005). Second, sounds of surrounding letters or words can influence each other.

In Figure 3.3, Emma spelled "friends" as "fanz" because she hears the "Z" at the end. Linguists have shown that "S" can fall into two categories:

Figure 3.3 A page from Emma's (5 years, 8 months) school journal.

voiced and voiceless. The voiced "S" as in "has," "is," and "his" takes a /z/ ending sound. The voiceless "S" as in "mess," "less," "yes," and "bus" has the conventional /s/ sound. When we pronounce "friends," we hear the voiced "S" or /z/. As experienced adults, we have acquired knowledge and experience over the years to know that "friends" ends with "S" although we hear /z/. "Dress," however, has the voiceless /s/, which Emma recorded with a single "S." Young children work out these types of sound–spelling relationships by inventing spelling forms. In the process, they write the sounds that they perceive, or what they think they hear.

At the same time, words generally do not occur in isolation of other words when speaking, which causes preceding sounds to influence what you perceive you hear. Emma's writing "playing dress up" as "plaen jras p" is an example. Emma dropped the "G" at the end of "playing" as "dress-up" became connected with "playing." In oral language, this type of spoken pattern is very common. Rarely do we fully articulate the "G" when other words follow. At the same time, within English phonology, the *dr-* in "dress-up" has evolved to sound like one phoneme that has the /j/ sound.

While we apply the English phonology, speakers of other languages apply their phonology to the Roman alphabet. The Roman alphabet is used by speakers of Spanish, French, German, and Italian. Its domination has been the effect of the power of the Roman Empire in preceding centuries. And while the Roman alphabet has relatively remained unchanged over the years, oral languages have evolved. As social and cultural beings, we have tried to merge a plethora of oral sounds to a limited number of letters. The benefit of the Roman alphabet is that it can accommodate the many sounds of the world's languages, and yet we fall in the danger of privileging certain orthographies over others.

Logo-Syllabic Sounds

Chinese and Japanese writing systems represent syllables. Chinese phonology is tonal, and, for instance, there are four tones to Chinese Mandarin: a high-level tone, a rising tone, a falling-rising tone, and a falling tone. Unlike English, there are a large number of Chinese characters with a few number of sounds including their tones. For instance, Rogers (2005) notes that the sound /yi/ can be written by at least 149 Chinese characters. Consequently, Chinese has a large number of homophones. Like a writer of English may switch "here" and "hear," a writer using Chinese characters may write a character that matches a particular sound but may not correspond to its meaning. Therefore, the semantic component of Chinese characters are critical in determining the meanings of words.

Consequently, although phonemes may change, the meaning always stays the same. In other words, Chinese characters are used in writing

Japanese and Chinese, but Japanese readers apply the Japanese phonology to Chinese characters. Therefore, while the pronunciation of any given character may change depending on the language, the meaning of the character stays the same.

Japanese phonology is built on a system of consonants and vowels. The core vowels in Japanese are "A," "E," "I," "O," and "U" (see Figure 3.2). Consonants are then added to the vowels, and words either end in a vowel or "N." Japanese incorporates two marks that change consonant sounds. The first mark is called a maru ({°}) and, for instance, alters the "P" to a "B." The second mark is called a ten-ten ({"}), which modifies the "T" to a "D." Overall, Japanese vowels sounds are used more consistently over consonants.

Like in Chinese, each Japanese symbol represents one syllable. For instance, the Japanese word "cat" (*neko*) is written in *hiragana* as ね こ There are two symbols: ね (*ne-*) and こ (*-ko*), one symbol for each syllable. This similar characteristic between Chinese and Japanese allows for effective incorporation of Chinese characters into Japanese writing. As in the Japanese sentence about buying ice cream, Japanese writers will use a Chinese character for one syllable and fill in the other syllables with *hiragana*. For instance, the Japanese infinitive "to eat" is 食べる (*taberu*). It has three syllables: *tabe-* (た べ) and *-ru* (る). The suffix *-ru* indicates that the verb is an infinitive form. In Japanese, the first syllable *ta-* is written with a Chinese character 食 and the second and third syllables are written in *hiragana* べる.

Internal Structure

This last point about writing systems is that they have an internal structure. Internal structure refers to how writing is organized separate from oral language (Rogers, 2005). I will briefly discuss two parts of internal structure: grammar and writing directionality.

Grammar

Grammar organizes the words that we put on the page, and it can be difficult to make sense of writing if we cannot make sense of the grammar. English is written in a subject–verb–object format, and subject–verb agreement is a cornerstone of conventional English grammar. English also has complex verb conjugations that relate to different verb forms. In addition, verbs can have objects (i.e. "ball" is the object in the sentence, "I threw the ball."). In English, there are a variety of prepositions, such as "in," "into," "by," and "through."

The main component of English grammar that tends to trouble many speakers of other languages such as Russian, Chinese, and Japanese are definite and indefinite articles (Bialystok & Hakuta, 1994). Many languages, such as Chinese and Japanese, do not have equivalents in their language for articles. For instance, while we say, "Please hand me the book," in Japanese the translated sentence would read, "Hon motte kite kudasai," with the direct English translation as "Hon [book] motte kite [bring me] kudasai [please]."

Chinese follows a similar subject–verb–object format, while Japanese verbs always appear at the end of the sentence. In addition, the subject does not have to appear in Japanese sentences. In the sentence above, "I" was inferred as the person who will buy the ice cream. Inclusion of the subject "I" allows the writer to emphasize who should buy the ice cream. Japanese does not possess plural forms of nouns. Multiple numbers of objects or people are indicated by adding a number in front of the noun.

Writing Directionality

In conventional English, text is written from left to right, starting at the top and moving down. Traditionally, Japanese was written starting at the top-right corner of the page. The writing progressed vertically to the bottom resulting in an individual writing from top to bottom, right to left. In more recent years, Japanese has taken a horizontal directionality in which writing always appears in a left-to-right directionality.

Multimedia and print in our communities have reinvented directionality in English. There are many instances when we see the word "hotel" written vertically in a top-to-bottom manner with flashing lights. At the same time, within Japanese magazines and newspapers, there are a variety of reading directionalities occurring on the same page. The title of an article may be written horizontally in a left-to-right directionality, while the text is read vertically right-to-left.

No matter the individual case, readers of any language are adept at making sense of directionality. More experienced readers learn the rules over time, and beginning early readers learn as they explore texts, try out different ways they should read, and recognize that particular directionalities cause the text to make more sense than others (Kabuto, 2005).

Learning to write across multiple writing systems, on the surface level, means navigating multiple written forms, becoming acquainted with phonology–orthography relationships, and developing an understanding of the internal structure of written languages. Emma did not necessarily have these categories of written language mastered by the time she was 7 years old. She did, however, demonstrate complex knowledge about the features of writing systems. In the following section, I will discuss and provide a model of how we can investigate the act of learning the characteristics of written languages by integrating a model of social practice. The goal is to explore how interweaving perspectives that combine developmental and linguistics factors that influence writing forms with social, cultural, and interpersonal influences can create more fully developed explanations that interweave the areas of language-in-use and sociocultural factors.

Writing across Languages from Multiple Perspectives

Emma (5 years, 4 months) and her father Jay were writing a New Year's card. Jay asked Emma to write "Happy New Year," "akemashite omedetou gozaimasu" on a piece of paper that he wanted to send to his parents who live in Japan.

Emma replied, "I can write Emma [in Japanese]."

"Zyaa, hitori de yatte nee." Jay replied that she should do it by herself.

Emma wrote her name on the card and proceeded to write "Happy New Year." Looking at the piece of paper on which her dad wrote the phrase in *hiragana*, Emma wrote "kemashite toozaima" (see Figure 3.4 for a comparison between Jay's and Emma's writings).

"How do you write 'o' [in Japanese *hiragana*]," she asked her father because she wanted to write "o" in front of "toozaima."

Holding and guiding Emma's hand to make a line horizontally, Jay said, "Bou o kaite." "Masugu itte, kuru," Jay continued as he guided her through the final stroke starting at the top and moving the pen down and around.

"Dekita." Emma said that she had done it. "I want to write more Japanese."

Emma took a piece of paper and asked her dad how to write "Christmas tree."

Phrase	Jay's Writing	Emma's Inventive Writing
Happy New Year ("Akemashite omedetou gozaimasu")	あけまして おめでとう ございます	けまして おどうざいも
Did you put up your Christmas tree? ("Kurisumasu tsuri-kazatta?")	クリスマスツリー かざった？	クリス マッツシリーかざった

Figure 3.4 Emma's (5 years, 4 months) inventive writing compared to Jay's conventional forms.

"Katakana de kakunakychya inkenai nee." Jay said that she needed to write it in *katakana*.

"Daddy kaite." Emma asked her father to write it for her, handing him a sheet of paper.

After her father finished writing a model for her on the paper, Emma wrote, "kurisumasu" on her sheet of paper. She continued to write "tsu" (ツ) in *katakana* and said, "That looks like a smiley face!"

Emma finished "tree," *tsuri*, and, handing him back the piece of paper, she asked her dad how to write *kazatta* (meaning "to put up the Christmas tree"). Jay wrote "kazatta" on the paper and handed it back to Emma.

Emma said, "I wonder if they put up a Christmas tree?" as she wrote the first two symbols for "ka" and "za."

"Look Daddy, you don't need [to say] the small 'tsu.' "

"Soo da nee." Her father replied that Emma was right. Emma finished writing "kazatta" and brought her paper to her dad.

What was Emma learning in the scenario above? How was she learning it? What was the role of her father in her learning? Did her talk and the written language play functions in her learning? Learning to write found its roots in social and cultural environments that shaped the ways that Emma used the linguistic aspects of language. From the dialogue above, writing in Japanese was not private knowledge that Emma learned independently. Instead, Japanese writing features became realized as they evolved out of a shared experience between Emma and her father as Jay guided the way in which Emma participated in this writing event. In this sense, two particular perspectives can be combined in order to highlight Emma's learning in this writing episode. The two theoretical perspectives involve learning as social practice and developmental, linguistic perspectives.

Learning as Social Practice

Learning as social practice is built on sociocultural theory that finds its roots in cultural psychology, which integrates the fields of anthropology and psychology (Gutierrez & Rogoff, 2003; Lave & Wenger, 1991; Vygotsky, 1986). Traditionally, psychology has focused on individual learning and universal aspects of learning processes and practices. Jean Piaget, as one of the more popular developmental psychologists, is an example of traditional psychology, or cognitive psychology. Cognitive psychology is ruled by experimentation and the discovery of individual processes and factors to learning. Piaget's explanations of egocentric thought and children's development through sensori-motor and concrete-operational thought are examples of how cognitive psychology is largely isolated from social and cultural environments (Piaget 1959; Piaget & Inhelder, 2000).

With the addition of anthropology, cultural psychology recognizes that our social and cultural environments play a large influence in our learning. Vygotsky (1986) writes that children's development is a child's "cultural development" in which learning is first the result of social (interpersonal) learning. Thus, Emma's learning in the above episode was the consequence of an interpersonal interaction between her and her father. The exchange of ideas and knowledge was shared through the use of cultural tools: oral language and writing forms. Here I will briefly explore how a sociocultural theory provides a foundation for discussing Emma's learning.

Children Are Active Members in Their Communities

In the above episode, Emma was aware of what she needed to know in order to be effective in writing in Japanese. When Emma needed to know how to write "O" and "Christmas tree," for instance, she approached her father, who she deemed as the more knowledgeable person. Emma played an active role by becoming a member within the family event. Emma initiated writing acts, such as writing her name in Japanese, or redirected acts, such as writing "Christmas tree" instead of "Happy New Year."

Emma's experience above supports a body of research that portrays how children help to create their learning contexts and learn about and how to use oral and written language through their social and cultural lives (Owocki & Goodman, 2002). Figure 3.5 provides another example of the social embeddedness of how literacy mediates relationships. The relationships, however, represented in Figure 3.5 were between Emma and her friends within a play context. Figure 3.5 is a contract that Emma (7 years,

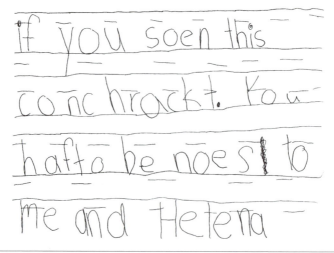

Figure 3.5 Emma (7 years, 5 months) wrote a contract to her friend Julianne.

5 months) wrote for her friend Julianne. On this particular play date at our house, Julianne was not listening to Emma and her other friend Helena, which Emma interpreted as Julianne being "mean." In trying to find a way to get Julianne to cooperate with them, Emma decided to design a contract. Gathering sheets of paper, Emma wrote the lines with a black colored pencil and wrote, "If you sign this contract, you have to be nice to me and Helena" in a red colored pencil. On another sheet of paper, Emma drew a straight line for Julianne's signature. In this particular example, Emma demonstrated sociocultural knowledge by recognizing that contracts were ways to take control of situations with a dynamic that was not in Emma's control.

Unstructured play provided Emma with a developmentally appropriate space where problem solving encouraged her to use oral and written languages (Owocki, 1999). Play, as Vygotsky (1986) suggests, provides a natural zone of proximal development where children can take risks and problem solve by relating previous knowledge to new situations. Vygotsky's notion of the zone of proximal development is created through social interactions and is a concept that allows us to visualize how Emma moved toward future learning through assistance. In these processes, Emma and other adults interacted with one another. In the writing episode above, Jay and Emma were working within a zone of proximal development in which Jay and Emma had both short- and long-term goals. In the short term, Jay and Emma wanted to complete the writing event. Emma's desire to write conventionally encouraged her to seek out her father's help. Although probably not realized at the time, Jay was co-constructing Emma's identity as a bilingual and biliterate person.

Family Members Mediate Children Learning through Guided Participation

In the writing episode above, we can see how Jay encouraged Emma to write her name when she expressed her ability to him. In addition, Jay wanted Emma to copy "Happy New Year" instead of writing it for her. Because Emma was a beginning reader and writer in both languages, Jay expected her to be able to exhibit those behaviors during the writing event, and his actions showed that he did not expect any less.

Jay guided and mediated the ways in which Emma participated in the activity (Rogoff, 2003). Because Jay was Emma's father and held a certain degree of control in these types of writing events, Emma did succumb to his requests. It is important, however, to recognize that Emma also employed her thoughts and actions, which were either accepted or rejected by her father, or me.

Guiding Emma's participation became realized in several different ways. First, Jay or I may have helped Emma make connections between old and new situations. For instance, when Jay wanted to help Emma understand something she read, he would say, "Remember when . . ." In addition, Jay or I "raised the bar" as Emma exhibited more competent behaviors (Rogoff & Gardner, 1984). Asking Emma to write her name herself instead of writing it for her is an example of how Jay and I raised the bar in Emma's learning.

Immediate scaffolding approaches were also utilized within reading and writing episodes to guide Emma's participation. Scaffolding approaches are like training wheels. There is some type of assistance given in order for Emma to reach her goals. Jay's holding of Emma's hand as he guided and talked her through the strokes for "O" is a scaffolding technique. Many of these guiding techniques may happen at once.

Blending of Practices

Every child's literacy learning is unique. In the excerpt above, enculturation into literacy was distinctive. Because English and Japanese were used in the home, both languages were mediating activities. Emma had books written in English and Japanese scripts and discovered ways in which these languages could provide her membership into multiple linguistic communities.

Consequently, Emma's growing up in a bilingual home blended language and literacy practices. Syncretic literacy studies suggest that children will take cultural and linguistic forms from their families and communities to create new language and literacy forms (Gregory et al., 2004). Emma's code switching in the writing episode, as well as in Chapter 2, was not the result of incomplete knowledge about language but was instead a strategic way of maneuvering the conversation that utilized and valued English and Japanese (Gort, 2006; Reyes, 2004).

A blending of biliterate practices can present itself in two ways: through literacy events and literacy practices. A literacy event is the observable act of reading and writing. It has often been the starting point for any unit of analysis because we can see it, talk about it with another person, or record it on video or audiotape; it is a tangible "thing." In the episode above, the event unfolded through the crafting process of Emma's New Year's card, how she formed the scripts, who or what she resourced, and what languages she used. Furthermore, the writing event occurred alongside code switching within speech events.

The literacy practice is the more general practice related to the literacy event. For instance, writing a New Year's card is a different type of practice than filling out a homework worksheet. Literacy practices are culturally embedded within our lives, and those who live cross-cultural lives merge these practices in order to participate with other people. For instance,

Christmas cards are not popular in Japan, and instead, New Year's cards are the customary greetings to send. In our house, we would first print out one set of holiday cards with "Merry Christmas." Emma observed us and participated in (as the episode above illustrates), transforming these cards into Japanese holiday cards by writing "Happy New Year" in *hiragana* on them.

There is a connection between a literacy practice and event. The literacy event results in a "thingness" that gives our experiences a concrete reality (Wenger, 1998). The things that we produce or read reify our experiences and help to define who we are; we connect with other people or with ourselves. The resources in our culture sometimes force us to transform, modify or blend practices to accommodate the range of literacy practices in our lives.

A sociocultural perspective helps us in understanding how social and cultural influences frame the ways we learn, but we still do not have the entire picture. For instance, a sociocultural perspective helps in understanding the ways in which Jay guided Emma's participation through the zone of proximal development, the identities that Emma and Jay negotiated in Emma's learning to write, and the discourses that were involved within the writing episode. The same pertains to Emma's contract in Figure 3.5. However, we do not have a way of discussing the actual text that was produced within the literacy event through a sociocultural framework. How do we analyze Emma's written text? For instance, Emma wanted to copy "Happy New Year," and copied it as "kemashite toozaima" instead of "akemashite omedetou gozaimasu." Consequently, we need another piece of the puzzle in discussing how Emma learned to write in multiple written languages.

Developmental, Linguistic Perspective

Developmental perspectives suggest that learning to read and write progresses in stages (Ferreiro & Teberosky, 1982; Kamii & Manning, 2002). Adding a biological notion to learning, children are seen as moving through their understandings of what reading and writing should look like. While children's invented reading and writing may progress through phases where they show particular developmental stages such as writing with strings of letters with no letter–sound correspondence to reading and writing initial consonants, caution should be taken in regarding reading and writing stages as static, stepwise progressions. At the same time, there are developmental, or what Owocki and Goodman (2002) call personal, influences that interplay with social and cultural forces. Instead, developmental factors have the possibility to frame the ways in which children interpret the forms and functions of reading and writing.

Invention/Convention

Goodman and Goodman (1990) coined the interplay of development and social and cultural forces as the interplay of personal invention and social convention. Owocki and Goodman argue that "internal and social forces work together to shape their [children's] understandings" (2002: 4). Likewise, Emma worked at her current developmental understandings of written marks, or personal inventions, which she demonstrated through her attempts at reading and writing. While Emma invented written language forms and spellings, she also tried to make cards, books, or personal letters look like their conventional form. Emma's contract shows that she not only invented word spellings but also creatively fashioned a contract by making it look official with lines and a place to sign. Emma's resourcefulness illustrates the knowledge she has about the discourses and practices of contract writing.

There were times when development did not always coincide with Emma's understanding of social convention. As Piaget argued (Piaget & Inhelder, 2000), Emma needed to assimilate new information to make it fit her current understanding. The process of assimilating means that Emma modified the information that she saw and accommodated it in her current schemata. This give and take of assimilating and accommodating can cause tensions between personal invention and social convention (Owocki & Goodman, 2002). A good example of these types of tensions occurred when Emma was in First Grade and did not want to write unless she knew how to spell correctly. She understood that words have conventional spellings but she was developmentally not able to reenact all the complexities of the English phonology–orthography relationships. As a result, she developed a short-lived resistance toward writing, and reading.

Role of Approximations in Learning to Read and Write

Personal inventions played a role in Emma's learning to read and write. Owocki and Goodman write, "What an adult assumes to be erroneous often reflects development in the child. Children's expressions of language, or inventions, reflect their current schemas, or working models for how language works" (2002: 4). In other words, Emma's inventions, or miscues, were windows into her perceptions, understandings, and beliefs about language.

Naturally, social environments played a role in valuing or devaluing Emma's inventions. Emma's writing episode above illustrates that Emma understood that there were conventional ways to write in Japanese. While Emma searched them out, she was not overly concerned with writing accurately. Her invented phrase for "Happy New Year" looks similar to the conventional phrase, and she recorded the majority of sounds in the phrase. Emma was encouraged to explore writing systems as she made approximations through personal inventions to written language features. If the social environment was not conducive to exploration, then Emma may have become overly concerned with accuracy in reading and writing rather than exploration.

Summary

A growing body of research acknowledges that we need to cross theoretical domains to discover deeper explanations of learning processes (Barton & Tusting, 2005; Taylor & Yamasaki, 2006). Others may argue that bringing in other perspectives weakens the theoretical foundation of our work. Critical examination of the whole child necessitates addressing the social, cultural, emotional, and linguistic domains of language and literacy. If theory cannot acknowledge that learning is first and foremost about who we are as humans, then theory, any theory, becomes dogmatic.

Emma acquired extensive knowledge in learning to be biliterate. She simultaneously learned about sociocultural knowledge and the characteristics of writing systems. The idea that she merely copied or passively acquired this knowledge is inaccurate. Emma was an active participant in every aspect of her learning. Through personal inventions, she explored written language forms, the phonology–orthography relationships in English and Japanese, and the internal structure of written languages.

These writing features were a means for Emma to build sociocultural knowledge about oral and written languages. In the writing episode, Emma learned that "Christmas tree" (a Western concept) is written in *katakana*. Through interactions with her family and community, Emma began to connect that writing is more than producing accurate forms. Instead, she started to establish the importance of selecting certain scripts in communicating ideas. Thus, the connection between social and cultural experiences and linguistic knowledge became a matrix that framed how she learned and what she learned. Keeping this point in mind, in the following chapters I will delve into the specifics of what and how Emma became biliterate by tying in written language forms, which will be the focus of the next chapter, with identity in Chapter 5. Chapter 6 will continue the discussion with identity, but with reading and oral language forms related to code switching.

Reaction Questions

Examine Figure 3.4 and the accompanying dialogue. Find examples of:

- Emma and Jay working in the zone of proximal development;

- Emma's active participation in creating written language;
- blending of language forms;
- personal inventions, or approximations.

Suggested Activities

1. Go on a literacy dig where you collect books, pamphlets, posters, and magazines from different writing systems. Children should be encouraged to bring in things from home. Have children compare the writing systems and outline the three features: written language forms, phonology and orthography, and internal structure.

2. Observe a literacy event where a child is writing in multiple languages. Analyze the event for the following:
   - the literacy practice;
   - the social context;
   - the developmental and linguistic factors;
   - the blending of language forms.

3. Using the literacy event in (2), try to find other theoretical perspectives that would provide insights into your observations. Some suggested theories are:
   - semiotic theory;
   - sociolinguistic theory;
   - sociocultural, historical perspectives on identity;
   - critical theory;
   - new literacy studies.

CHAPTER 4

Writing and Drawing as Active Discovery

In this chapter, I will explore Emma's inventive representations as windows into her growing understandings of the forms and organization of written Japanese and English. I will first introduce the idea of writing and drawing attributes. In the latter part of the chapter, I will discuss the relationships between writing and drawing forms for the reason that drawing dominated Emma's early self-created samples in the home, and to leave drawing out of the discussion would provide an incomplete picture of the modes that Emma found meaningful in her early representations. Another reason for examining the relationships between writing and drawing aids is acknowledging the flexibility that Emma demonstrated as she moved across writing and drawing forms.

Representation of Attributes in Writing and Drawing Forms

Emma's early writing and drawing possessed representational attributes, which are key identifying features of an object. The attributes that Emma used were initially based on size, shapes, and lines, and the more experienced Emma became with written forms the more her attention to attributes increased, which in turn allowed her to visually move across written language forms. In this way, Emma was not directly taught all the written forms of Japanese and English. Instead, discovery through the physical transformation of written marks led to an awareness and attention to detail that allowed Emma to make visual connections between written forms and drawing.

Attributes in Writing and Drawing Forms

To illustrate, Figure 4.1 is an example of the way Emma employed attributes to create meaningful objects. Emma (3 years, 4 months) drew Figure 4.1 as the second page of a book that she made by stapling paper together. Emma said that she drew balloons, which were drawn in orange, purple, yellow, green, red, brown, and beige. Emma's balloons possess two major attributes: the colored circles (the balloon) and the straight line (the string tied to the balloon).

Emma's attention to attributes also occurred in creating writing forms. For instance, on the first page of Emma's book, she wrote Figure 4.2 on which she wrote the letters "T," "P," "E," "P," "T," and "A." The attributes that represent the letters are similar to those that made the balloons: circles and lines. The letters are composed of lines oriented in a manner that creates an image of alphabetic letter form. The "P," however, is slightly different. Emma wrote "P" with two attributes and connected them

Figure 4.1 Emma (3 years, 4 months) drew balloons on the second page of her book.

Figure 4.2 Emma wrote the letters "T," "I," "E," and "A" on the second page of her book.

together which made them look like a balloon shape only that they are not colored. Emma's "P" resembles both a letter and a drawing form. In the context of other letters, the form is visually letter-like.

When exploring writing forms, Emma's attention to and use of attributes suggests that she did not need to be taught all the conventional forms of written English and Japanese. Instead, Emma cultivated a flexibility in creating new forms by experimenting with adding or subtracting attributes from existing letter forms. For instance, Emma learned that she could add a line to the left side of a circle and make a "P" without being directly instructed to do so. In addition, thinking about the ordering of the figures, Emma wrote Figure 4.2 before she drew the balloons in Figure 4.1. It is plausible that Emma drew the balloons after the "P" because they were visually similar. By drawing balloons after writing Figure 4.2, Emma may have been attempting to create differentiation between the two forms: a drawing and a writing form, a point that I will come back to later in the chapter.

Attributes to Write across Scripts

Emma's visual flexibility in generating modified forms between English and Japanese scripts is illustrated in Figure 4.3. When I initially came across Figure 4.3, I was perplexed as to what Emma was trying to do.

Figure 4.3 Emma (3 years, 5 months) created a script using attributes of the Roman alphabet and Japanese *hiragana*.

Figure 4.3 was written on the top portion of a piece of paper and the bottom portion had large, overlapping circular and vertical lines. Since I did not directly observe Emma writing Figure 4.3, I asked her about it; at 3 years, 5 months of age, she could only tell me that she "wrote letters and drew lines." My immediate attention was given to the portion of lines and semicircles that made the letter forms "R," "B," "K," "H," and "A." At the same time, I noticed the other semicircular marks intersecting with horizontal lines. When I started to break Emma's invented forms into attributes, Table 4.1 emerged. In fact, as Table 4.1 illustrates, Emma's invented forms possess attributes linked to alphabetic letters and Japanese *hiragana*.

By adding pieces such as semicircles or crossed lines, Table 4.2 outlines Emma's invented forms carry pieces of Roman and Japanese *hiragana* scripts. For instance, if we take Emma's "K" with the circle on the vertical line, Emma's form visually relates to "K," "T," "O," and "R" within the Roman alphabet. At the same time, there are related forms to eight *hiragana* symbols. When I examined scripts in this manner, what seemed unusual before was no longer perplexing. By looking for common attributes and perceptually rearranging these attributes, I sensed how Emma's marks were the consequence of meaningfulness and purposeful actions.

Back in Chapter 2, I described Emma's first collected Japanese writing sample, on which she wrote the *kanji* for rain, *ame*, at 3 years, 6 months (see Figure 2.1), which was the only Japanese that Emma wrote until 4 years, 3 months. Neither Jay nor I directly taught her *kanji*, and she did not copy it from a book or magazine, although she must have had some familiarity with it. In addition, before she wrote the *kanji*, Emma wrote her name and strings of letters. Looking closely at sequence of her writing, I do not believe that it was happenstance that Emma discovered the *kanji*. Table 4.2 illustrates how all the previous letter forms have attributes that belong to the *kanji*.

Table 4.1 The connection between Emma's invented forms and English and Japanese *hiragana* scripts.

Emma's Invented Writing Form	Attributes of the Form	Relationship to English	Relationship to Japanese
		B P O	あ は ほ
		K T O R	た ち け さ ね ま は ほ
		H L	し け せ に は ほ
		A T O	た あ は ほ

Emma started out with "E," and her "E" flipped on its side is the bottom base for *ame*. Emma wrote a series of "A"s, which could also become the base. The letter "F" has the potential to become the top part of *ame*. Immediately before Emma wrote the full *kanji*, she again wrote "A." In essence, Emma already had all the pieces of the *kanji* on her paper. Emma generated a new form by repositioning or visually modifying standard forms (Clay, 1975). Through her physical action and perceptual flexibility, Emma discovered that she could transform marks into English and Japanese scripts.

Table 4.2 Emma's sequence in writing before she wrote the *kanji* for rain.

Emma's Writing Forms	Attribute of the Form	Connection to a Another Script

Connections between Writing and Drawing

Inarguably, both writing and drawing forms were important modes of communicating meaning in Emma's early representations, and her early marks show that she differentiated the forms of writing and drawing. Figure 4.4 illustrates Emma's inventive writing at 3 years, 5 months of age. On a piece of stationery, Emma wrote these letter-like forms and read it

Figure 4.4 Emma (3 years, 5 months) wrote circles and semicircles in a sequential manner and read it as "Dear Mommy."

as "Dear Mommy." While the letter-like forms have attributes in the forms of lines and circles (half and full), they are also controlled marks and linear to make them look like written language. Compared to the first sample I collected at 2 years, 1 month (see Timeline), the lines and circles in Figure 4.4 are localized and singular rather than encompassing the entire page and repeated, or multiple. The lines in each of the two examples required different physical movements and perceptual arrangements.

Both writing and drawing are made up of repeated movement (Clay, 1975). Figure 4.4 illustrates the repetitive nature of writing in that, with the exception of the "H," Emma wrote based on some derivative of an "O," which caused her to use similar, recurring strokes. Drawing is also composed of repeated movement, and Figure 4.1 is an example of how the repetition of physical movements was used to draw images. In both cases, Emma created multiple versions of similar marks. These recurring movements result in similar attributes that made up the writing and drawing forms in Figure 4.1 and Figure 4.3.

For instance, in Figure 4.5, Emma wrote the letters in her name in brown on the top of the page and then rotated the page to write the circles and lines in the middle. Emma said that the objects in the middle of the page were the letter "P," and, using words that one would normally apply to images, commented that the "P" has "one circle and one line."

On the other hand, in Figure 4.6, Emma wrote "O," "U," and "E" and drew a face. When she drew the face, she commented, "Look, the eyes and nose are Os." Emma linked circular letters with the attributes of a face. In this example, through drawing, Emma labeled pieces of the images using letters. Throughout her early writing years, Emma connected drawing forms and English and Japanese scripts. Back in Chapter 3, when Emma wrote "Christmas tree" in *katakana*, she said that ツ (*tsu*) looks like a smiley face. Even at a later age, the boundaries of what constituted a writing form and an image were permeable. In other words, Emma linked forms that made up writing and those of drawing.

While Emma linked writing and drawing attributes together, she defined writing and drawing by actively generating attributes to redefine, or differentiate, writing and drawing forms. In Figure 4.7, Emma wrote "Mommy" and her name. Emma wrote her "A" under the "M." After writing "Mommy" and "Emma," on the bottom-left corner, she wrote an "O" inside another "O." After she completed the sign, Emma said that an "O" inside another "O" looks like a doughnut. Emma described her sign to me by reading and pointing to "Mommy" and "Emma." Emma read the bottom line as "doughnut, A, O, O." I find it interesting that the two "O"s between the two "A"s are different sizes but are not inside one

Figure 4.5 Emma (3 years, 3 months) wrote her name, "E," "A," and "P," which she described as having a circle and a line.

Figure 4.6 Emma (3 years, 2 months) discusses the face's features in terms of letters.

Figure 4.7 Emma (3 years, 4 months) added an "O" inside the larger "O," which made the form look like a doughnut.

another like in the doughnut. In this example, Emma realized that by adding variations to the letter "O" (through attributes), she transformed her writing to an image.

Figure 4.8 provides another example. When she brought it home, I asked her to tell me about her sign. Emma read three names: "Emma," "Mommy," and "Rika" (her Japanese-speaking friend) and said that she drew balloons. Created four months after Figure 4.1, Emma was still trying to discover ways to differentiate a letter from an image that carried the same attributes. Emma said that the balloons "looked like Ps," which caused her to color them to make them resemble balloons. Similar to Figure 4.1, Emma applied a similar attribute—the solid coloring inside the "P"—to differentiate the writing from the drawing.

While one dimension of differentiating writing and drawing related to attributes, another dimension addressed to the use of space. Emma applied a variety of spatial concepts that affected the visual orientations of writing and drawing (Kress, 1997). Take Figure 4.9 as an example. Emma (4 years, 3 months) drew three flowers and a tree and wrote her name in *hiragana*. The drawing forms take more space than the writing and tell a different story. The tree is an apple tree, and there are purple and yellow flowers covering the ground. Emma's name, although full of meaning

Figure 4.8 Emma (3 years, 8 months) added color to the "P"s to make them into balloons.

which I will elaborate on in the next chapter, is written in two *hiragana* symbols. The drawing contains more graphic details than the writing.

Some of Emma's earliest signs that included writing were graphically similar to images. She used a variety of colors to write and draw, and, as Figure 4.10 illustrates, Emma's letters are arranged spatially around the paper, and she used 12 different colors to create her sign. There were times when Emma's drawings were spatially organized, like writing. Figure 4.1 is such an example, in which Emma lined up her balloons in a linear manner as she did her letters in Figure 4.2.

Over time, Emma began to develop an understanding that drawing represents spatial concepts and writing is a sequential representation. I prefer the use of "sequential" over "linear" because the succession of letters is what drove Emma's writing. Emma was concerned with putting letters in a sequence, one letter after the other, rather than ensuring that the resulting word, sentence, or phrase held a linear reading directionality (horizontal and/or vertical). In Figure 4.7, where Emma wrote her name in a sequential manner but not in a linear orientation, the end product is spread out over two lines. Emma began to demonstrate the sequential orientation of writing as she became interested in connecting symbols to invent words.

Exploring the sequential orientation of words in English and Japanese allowed Emma to be flexible in writing directionality, which may not be similar to reading directionality. Unlike English, Japanese can be written

Figure 4.9 Emma (4 years, 3 months) demonstrates how writing and drawing represent different visual concepts.

from top to bottom or from left to right or both. Because Emma focused on the sequence of letters or Japanese symbols, she had the freedom to explore directionality in writing in both languages. Figure 4.11 is an example of English writing. In Figure 4.11, Emma wrote her friend Sara's name in a vertical direction: the "A" appears next to the "R" because she ran out of room at the bottom of the page.

In Figure 4.12, Emma (4 years, 3 months) wrote *tentomushi* ("ladybug") from top to bottom on the left side of the page and *momo* ("peach") from left to right. Regardless of the directionality, Emma composed both words by writing the Japanese *hiragana* symbols in a succession, with one symbol following the previous. These observations strongly suggest that Emma understood spatial directionality by understanding that words are sequential, while images are nonlinear and spatially composed.

Figure 4.10 Emma (3 years, 2 months) used writing to design a sign reminiscent of drawing.

Because I never asked Emma the question, "Which is writing?" and "Which is drawing?" it is difficult to know if Emma at this time understood the difference in the abstract concepts of writing and drawing. It is clear that she did acknowledge that there are particular features that distinguish the two. However, Emma's comments around her writing and drawing reveal that while her writing and drawing can be composed with similar strokes, they need to possess certain variations. These variations become highlighted through the details that defined her work and emerged in the form of attributes. And Emma explored the attributes of writing and drawing forms by thoroughly experimenting with her inventive marks. Upon reflection, I do not believe it is necessarily a matter of whether Emma differentiated the concepts of writing or drawing but instead a matter of how she came to understand that writing and drawing are made up of similar and different attributes; how

Figure 4.11 Emma (3 years, 6 months) wrote Sara's name in a horizontal manner.

they demanded different physical movements, and have certain "naming" vocabulary.

Writing as an Act of Discovery

Writing is an act of discovery that requires perceptual rearrangements and physical representations and always embedded in social and cultural contexts. To uncover the mystery of writing across multiple scripts, I needed to illustrate how the entirety of Emma's symbolic repertoires, framed by cultural settings, mutually constructed one another (Dyson, 2002). As writing, images, talk, and movement work together, I could not completely detach writing from its context to study it as an isolated phenomenon to draw comprehensive conclusions about Emma's developing writing abilities. Emma's early endeavors in written communication, while they do involve some developmental principles, evolved out of factors that cannot be listed in a checklist or universally tested. Emma cultivated a certain degree of perceptual flexibility through deep noticing to make links as she worked across modes. This ability came about as Emma efficiently employed physical and cultural tools within authentic contexts that promoted exploration.

Figure 4.12 In *hiragana*, Emma (4 years, 3 months) wrote *tentomushi* (ladybug) vertically and *momo* (peach) horizontally.

Perceptual Flexibility across Writing Scripts and Drawing Forms

Learning to write across scripts and to draw involved perceptual engagements with how Emma's inventive marks could reflect conventional written language forms. Growing up in a home that was full of graphic information, Emma was always looking and seeing, which was a constant endeavor and act. As a baby, she explored visual fields, reaching out for toys and using her hands to pick up objects, blankets, toys, or shoes. Emma's hands were the main instrument that linked the eyes with mental thought (Wilson, 1998). When Emma was able to handle writing tools and put pencil to paper, the marks that she made were exploratory as she tested out how the tools work. In other words, Emma needed to discover the benefits and limitations of writing tools, such as, for example, what would happen if she used a white crayon on white paper. Very little. Although Emma knew that the crayon had to have worked because she could use it on pink paper, the white paper limited the visual acuity of the marks.

Emma was building a history of perceptual understandings with every attempt at writing and drawing by collecting and applying new information about the general act of making marks. Perceptual learning necessitates a constant state of awareness during which Emma observed and examined written language around her and tried to give shape to what she saw and imagined in her mind (John-Steiner, 1985). Through developing an awareness of written language, Emma observed and extracted information in the form of what attributes define the written marks that she was observing. Emma may have observed that the Japanese *hiragana* is composed of circles and lines, and the circles can intersect the lines in the middle, whereas within the English alphabet, the circles appear at the top or the bottom of the lines in upper and lowercase letters (i.e. "P," "p," "B," or "b"). As Emma gathered defining attributes, she combined them to what she could write. These actions resulted in applying new perceptual patterns to previous information, which was illustrated in Figure 4.3 where Emma superimposed attributes that made up *hiragana* with alphabetic letters. By creating variation in forms, Emma was actively testing attributes, their properties and their potentialities within an organized system of written language.

These conclusions follow suit from other researchers studying beginning writing in languages such as Chinese (Lin, 2007) and Arabic (Baghban, 1984; Taylor et al., 2002). Insights into Emma's writing support these growing studies and suggest that young children interpret the forms of multiple written languages through a holistic lens. What this means is that, initially, Emma learned language from whole to part, which is the reason why she began to isolate the parts, or attributes, of written language forms. In other words, Emma did not see individual features of written forms separate from the whole of written language, or individual sounds separate from the entirety of oral language. To provide another example, Harste et al. (1984) presented an early writing sample completed by an Arabic-speaking 4-year-old child. Because the system of dotting and curlicue forms is pervasive within Arabic's written forms, the child filled her paper with curved lines and dots. When she finished her writing, Harste et al. quoted her as saying, "Here, but you can't read it, cause I wrote it in Arabic and in Arabic we use a lot more dots than you do in English" (1984: 82). In another example, Lin (2007) illustrated how a young Chinese-speaking child at 2 years, 6 months created writing forms by repeating strokes though overlapping individual marks, which made her marks look like Chinese characters.

Another dimension of perceptual flexibility related to the connection between writing forms in English and Japanese and drawing forms. As I have illustrated, Emma experimented with a variety of graphic forms. Combining Emma's growth as a writer and drawer, who designed an assortment of graphic objects, validates the symbolic repertoires of communication that supported her learning. Emma saw and used writing forms within her drawings; she found smiley faces in *katakana* and perceived the letter "O" in the faces that she drew. She also connected English scripts with *katakana* scripts. Emma once noted that the *katakana* { ⊥ } looks like the Roman "I." These mental linkages between forms allowed her to work across a variety of scriptal possibilities and created a perceptual flexibility in connecting entire forms across scripts or drawing. Emma tried to find significance in what she crafted and what she viewed within those graphic designs. By saying that a *katakana* { ⊥ } looks like the alphabetic "I," Emma actively searched for and developed coherence among written forms of Japanese and English and drawing. And yet, as she searched for a cohesive understanding of written marks, she looked, noticed, and discovered patterns to note individual differences. Emma's experiences contend that differences among Japanese and English written forms are not inherently a source of difficulty.

Authentic Discovery

Emma's writing was spontaneous. In some ways, it arose out of self-discovery about what she could do and how she could do it. And it was always embedded within a context that promoted ways in which Emma could actualize the internal representations of graphic forms to external realities. Emma did not learn to write in multiple languages through rote memorization and drills; she learned to write in Japanese and English because social driving forces created an authentic and natural means for composing signs. Emma's contract to Julianne, her letter to me, and writing her friend's Sara's name were ways in which texts shaped Emma's experiences in the home, defined her friends, and developed relationships with other people.

Emma acted out of her personal interest when she wanted to create signs. Personal interest was a liberating act where individuality intersected with social action. Liberation infers that Emma could write particular identities and portray herself as a biliterate child. Social action relates to the notion that Emma could, as a biliterate child, challenge the social constraints of an English-dominant society and expand her competences as a writer.

At the same time, Emma played with language. My use of the word "play" refers to serious and complex work on behalf of any child. Emma's writing "T" and "O," her letters with added attributes, and her *kanji* for *ame* did not have an immediate social purpose. Writing for herself, Emma interacted with writing features, and the result was discovery. Whereas a social orientation toward writing encouraged Emma to develop relationships with other people, she also played with writing forms. These factors set up an authentic context where Emma could seriously and purposefully investigate how writing systems work.

Summary

Emma learned about the forms of written languages as she looked and noticed different attributes that made up scripts. This work involved learning to see and approximate the details that differentiate writing forms in English and Japanese. Learning to write details entails active exploration of a variety of communicative forms in meaningful contexts around both physical and cultural tools.

Emma's discoveries were not linear in any way and reoccurred when she tried to invent forms. Writing was more about authentic discovery than about documenting developmental and conventional writing. At 3 years, 2 months, Emma wrote conventional "to-ot," and one month later invented the letter "P" with circles with lines that dissected the "O," resulting in a form that did not immediately resemble a letter. Emma wrote "Mommy" at 3 years, 4 months but wrote letter-like forms and read it as "Dear Mommy" at 3 years, 5 months in Figure 4.4.

Tracking Emma's developmental evolution from lines to letters or drawing to writing was a difficult task because of the degree of fluctuation in her conventional writing for the reason that there are many factors involved in the social context that are not included in developmental stages. As Vygotsky's quote that opened Emma's biliteracy timelines states, Emma never lost one aspect to gain another. When children write in an authentic context, writing becomes spontaneous and not a unidirectional process. Children's immediate personal and vested interests inject their role in their writing as much as developmental factors. The movement toward writing in multiple languages is multifaceted. Emma learned the forms of written language and she learned about herself in relation to others. In this sense, writing is also a discovery of identity.

Reaction Questions

Return to Emma's biliteracy timeline. Can you find evidence of developmental writing? Can you find evidence of spontaneous writing?

Suggested Activities

1. Observe a young child write or draw. Document what the child does to compose the writing or drawing. Describe the writing or drawing:
   - through the use of attributes;
   - through how the child adds or subtracts lines to distinguish writing and drawing forms;

- through how the child uses recurring marks and through the use of space.
2. Ask an early biliterate child to pretend to write in English and their native language. Find differences and similarities in their interpretation of writing forms.

CHAPTER **5**

Early Writing as Social Practice

The Self in Action

This chapter continues the discussion on Emma's writing. Whereas the previous chapter introduced Emma's visual and physical explorations of writing, this chapter extends the connection of writing to human action. Human action in this chapter portrays writing as a means for Emma to act upon her world—to develop or change relationships, or to challenge or support the social spaces within which she participated (Dyson, 1993; Gee, 2002). Once Emma began to experiment with the written forms of Japanese and English, she set out on an endeavor to appreciate the possibilities and potentialities of writing in developing a sense of herself in relation to other people and social structures. What I want to emphasize is that control of written language did not precede the ways in which it could be used for social action. These two aspects went hand in hand; one developed the other.

To illustrate this point, this chapter will discuss bilingual writing in relation to identity. The first part of the chapter will propose that Emma developed her social and language identities through the concepts of self-authoring through available scripts. The latter part of the chapter will specifically examine how writing voice and scripts were tied to social spaces to illustrate how bilingual writing is an act of identity.

Authoring the Self

The more Emma exhibited competent abilities as a writer of English and Japanese, the more people commented on her language capabilities. There were times when her friends would ask her to write something in Japanese or to say something in Japanese. Those of us who are bilingual ourselves are not immune to these types of requests from others. Emma also heard my friends' comments that it was admirable that Emma could read and write in both languages. Needless to say, there were times when Emma felt proud that she was growing up bilingual and biliterate.

Figure 5.1 was the result of one of these occurrences. Emma (5 years, 5 months) created Figure 5.1 for a family friend who was monolingual English-speaking and who often openly commented on the value of Emma's use of Japanese. In the figure, Emma drew two flowers and the sun and wrote "Emma and Rick and" on the top line and "Shimajiro and Mimirin, Blanket, and Rika and" on the second row, all in *hiragana*. Although Emma wanted to write in *hiragana*, she did not have control of all the aspects of Japanese, and, to overcome this point, Emma searched out a *hiragana* chart as a model for the *hiragana* symbols. Even with the use of the chart, her writing illustrates pieces of her personal invention. In particular, the -*ma* in "Emma" (the second symbol on the first line) and the -*ma* in Shimajiro (the second symbol on the second line) show a different physical movement that resulted in a mirror image of

Figure 5.1 Emma (5 years, 5 months) wrote in *hiragana* "Emma and Rick and" on the top line and "Shimajiro and Mimirin, Blanket, and Rika and" on the bottom line.

the *hiragana* "ma": the first rotates clockwise, while the second rotates counterclockwise.

On the one hand, Figure 5.1 illustrates the symbiotic relationship between developing control of written forms and the social context within which Emma's writing and her desire to write were embedded. Little explanation is needed around the fact that Emma wanted to show her Japanese writing abilities. And yet, by demonstrating that she could physically write in Japanese, what was Emma actually portraying about herself as a bilingual writer?

First, Emma highlighted her voice as a writer or the notion that as an individual who had unique and personal perspectives and interests, she was a participant in webs of social life (Holquist, 1981). In other words, Emma's voice was not singular but pluralistic as she brought in Discourses (with the big "D"; see Gee, 1996) from different social domains of practice. For instance, in Figure 5.1 Emma combined pieces of Japanese childhood items to family and friends to create a self-portrait. Shimajiro and Mimirin were characters from a Japanese storybook, Emma and Rick are siblings in a bilingual family, *mofu* was Emma's blanket which was given to her by her Japanese grandmother, and Rika was Emma's Japanese friend. The common thread among the intersecting domains connected to Japanese language and culture. Figure 5.1 was about Emma because it was through the orchestration of these words and voices that Emma could communicate something about herself.

In addition, as a bilingual writer, Emma illustrated the process by which she synchronized the social languages that shaped who she was in relation to other people or practices through self-authoring (Holland et al., 1998; Holquist, 1981). As I mentioned earlier, Emma used images and four scripts in her self-produced writing samples. Researchers have argued that individual scripts should be viewed as particular modes (Kenner & Kress, 2003). For instance, *kanji, hiragana, katakana,* and the Roman alphabet are separate modes rather than one mode (writing) for the reason that modes are an organized means of representation. *Katakana* is used for borrowed words, which encourages writers of Japanese to select *katakana* over *hiragana* or *kanji* in certain instances. Similarly, Emma may have strategically selected particular scripts that served specific purposes, such as writing in English when addressing her English-speaking friends or in *hiragana* to write to her grandparents. The choices that Emma made were thoughtful reflections of how scripts would be received by her audience and aligned herself into larger social structures of home and community.

Finally, Figure 5.1 displays how Emma's writing was dialogic, meaning that there were at least two (if not more) voices directly involved (Holquist, 1981). Unlike speech in which Emma could receive an immediate response with another person, she needed to presuppose the response that she would have received from the audience to whom she was writing. For instance, by writing in Japanese in Figure 5.1, Emma conjectured that she would get a positive response, such as "Wow, you wrote in Japanese for me!" or "That's great! Tell me about what you wrote." The relationship between the addressee and the addresser is known as dialogism. One voice relates to who is doing the speaking, and the other refers to who is being addressed. In Figure 5.1, Emma was the one who was doing the authoring. At the same time, she needed to presuppose the voice of her audience, which also influenced the ways in which she wanted to write (Wertsch, 1991).

This process is not as straightforward as it may seem. For instance, if Emma presupposed the voice of her audience for Figure 5.1, she could have easily written the same words in the Roman alphabet, which she did in other signs. However, while she may have addressed the audience, she probably would have altered the meaning of her sign. The script was just as important in communicating her biliterate identity as many of the words she selected. Having the option to select from different scripts provided Emma with flexibility in communicating meaning through written languages. Emma needed to make decisions on what she wanted to communicate, how she wanted to express herself, and what her audience would take from the sign.

In this sense, writing involves understanding yourself in relation to others. This notion is what I will call identity. As I described in Chapter 2, identity is a complex idea. Naturally, we have physical characteristics that help in defining who we are, or biological aspects that align us to particular social and cultural groups. Nonetheless, we socially construct who we are by interacting with others. We acquire particular ways of speaking, dressing, writing, and acting. These "things" that begin to tag how we present ourselves make up our identity toolkit (Gee, 1996). For Emma, being able to write in four scripts became part of her toolkit. From here, I will explore the ways scripts provided Emma with a means of writing her identity through her name writing and script switching.

Name Writing

Emma's ability to recognize the connection between the meaning of her spoken and written names heralded an important early literacy milestone (Clay, 1975; Haney, 2002). Emma's name provided her with a meaningful vehicle to learn reading and writing skills. This observation is not new to the field of early literacy, and the study of young children's name writing dates back to 1936 with the work of Hildreth, who studied children's developmental progressions and sequences in conventional name writing. Hildreth (1936) focused on the use of horizontal and vertical lines, the movement toward formed letters, the ability to use spaces, and conventional name spellings.

Name writing allowed Emma to build on personally meaningful information in her early years. Emma's initial encounter with name writing was writing in English. Name writing was one of her first labels (Baghban, 2007), and, as the biliteracy timeline illustrates, the first letter that she wrote was the letter "E" at 2 years, 11 months, which she wrote with a crayon and painted with a paintbrush. Until Emma's full name appeared at 3 years, 2 months, Emma read the letter "E" as Emma. Emma also demonstrated what researchers have called the name–letter effect, meaning that Emma preferred the letters in her own names over other letters (Haney, 2002). Emma's early name-writing behaviors support a plethora of research that highlights how name writing provides venues for children to recognize letters and understand letter sounds, relationships between phonology and orthography, and print concepts (Haney, 2002; Owocki & Goodman, 2002).

Dynamic Nature of Name Writing

While Emma's name writing fell into certain developmental factors particularly with her name writing in English, there was also a dynamic nature. In addition, to labeling the "E" as Emma at her first attempts to write her name, Emma first wrote her name in a nonlinear manner, although it was sequential, until the age of 3 years, 4 months, when Emma wrote her name in a linear fashion. The dynamic nature of Emma's growth in representing her name means that "name writing as a developmental process" should be examined through the idea that Emma absorbed information in her environment and actively transformed it (Ferreiro, 1986). Ferreiro argued that development is not synonymous with "a succession of accomplishments" or a "restful traveling from one stage to another" (1986: 48). Instead, to evolve into literacy means that Emma needed to work with what she knew at a given point in time. To illustrate this point, Emma's biliteracy timeline shows that she first wrote her name in *hiragana* when she was 4 years, 3 months old (see Figure 5.2). This observation was not coincidental. Emma wrote her name in *hiragana* the same month that she received the storybook *Shimajiro* in which the main character is learning about writing in *hiragana*.

Resources such as *Shimajiro* opened doors for writing in *hiragana*. Now, Emma could select either the Roman alphabet or *hiragana* to write her name and her Japanese-speaking friends' names. By receiving information from her environment, Emma expanded her repertoire in representing herself and others.

Figure 5.2 Emma (4 years, 3 months) wrote her name in *hiragana*.

Figure 5.3 Emma (5 years, 2 months) became upset when she could not write "E" in *hiragana*.

Yet, when Emma was 5 years, 2 months old, she suddenly became upset when she could not write her name in *hiragana*. I found Figure 5.3 on the floor and immediately asked Emma what she wrote. Emma said, "I wrote 'Ema mo' " and began to cry. When I inquired into why she was crying, Emma replied, "Because I couldn't write 'e' [in *hiragana*]." I suggested to Emma that she should ask her father for help. Bringing a piece of paper and a pen to her father, Jay provided Emma with the strokes to make the hiragana "E."

On his knees at the coffee table and Emma on his lap, Jay said, "Chyon. Yooko ni boo hite," as he guided Emma's hand to make the top horizontal ("chyon") and vertical lines ("yooko ni boo hite") of "E."

Continuing to guide her hand down sideways, Jay said, "Naname ni oroshite." Then he followed, "Naname ni agate. Guru guru." Jay told Emma to go up sideways and make a wavy line.

"Zyaa. 'Ma' jiibun de yatte mite." Jay wanted Emma to try -*ma* on her own.

Emma wrote "ma" and quickly brought it to me. "Look Mommy. I wrote Emma." Emma then drew circles around her name and the flower at the bottom (see Figure 5.4).

Emma's experience is common among many children. She appeared to "know it" one day but not the next. The reason for this observation is that learning is dynamic and Emma had to manage, organize, and make sense

Figure 5.4 Emma's father helped Emma to write "E" in *hiragana* and encouraged her to write *ma* independently.

of different types of input from her environment. She saw things that she did not see before, which required her to adjust her working schemata. Emma knew that her personal invention in Figure 5.3 somehow looked like the conventional form. In fact, she represented two attributes (the top mark and the bottom portion) of the *hiragana* "E." Coincidentally, Emma represented attributes that visually resemble the Roman alphabet ("H") and *hiragana* ("N" and "E"). In Piagetian terms, Emma was in a state of disequilibrium.

In order to move out of this state, Emma turned to her father as a guide. Jay provided Emma with the information that she needed to be successful but at the same time allowed her to demonstrate some of her own name-writing skills. In other words, Emma's figures suggest that writing development denotes a movement out of states where current knowledge comes in conflict with what one sees or understands from their social worlds.

Names as Personal Property

Children find that their names make them distinct from other people (Haney, 2002). Emma made comments such as "She has my E," or, if she came across another Emma, "She has my name." Indignant that other people could have pieces of or her entire name, Emma developed a possession of her name as solely tied to herself. Naturally, as Emma became older, she learned that people may have the same name, but this was not a quick concept that Emma accepted. The reason is that name writing linked to Emma's sense of self; it became personal property of the owner.

Name Writing and Identity

More recent work in name writing addresses how names are closely tied to identity, family, and culture (Haneda, 2005; Thompson, 2006). Research on binominal identities has opened a rich area of study for understanding the complexities between one's sense of self and assimilation into multiple cultural groups. Thompson (2006) argues that names carry social currency and that linguistically diverse groups invest in personal names in order to gain access into social contexts. Many individuals who immigrate into the USA forgo their given name for an "American" one as my mother did back in the 1970s when she came to the USA with my father, supporting Thompson's claim that "an investment in a personal name is an investment in social identity" (2006: 190).

While this case is one particular type of name investment, there are also others. With our globalized society, movement between countries is increasing. Transnational families are an example of how families are adopting to easier and less expensive travel in order to maintain lives across countries. In addition, through advanced technology, transnational families are able to maintain close ties to families back in native countries through video phones and chats, something that was not possible 20 years ago.

At the time of Emma's birth, our family was an example of a transnational family. Emma was born in Tokyo while we were temporarily there for Jay's work. While Jay's family, who we visited frequently, was in Japan, my family was in the USA. During the first two years of Emma's life we traveled back to the USA three times. Jay and I wanted to maintain emotional, linguistic, and cultural ties to both our family in Japan and in the USA. In order to keep this connection, Jay and I decided to give Emma a name that would allow her to live among both cultural worlds.

Emma as a Multinominal Name

Emma's name contains phonetic sounds which are present in both English and Japanese although it may be considered more of an anglophone name than a Japanese one. Particularly with the influence of English and the Romanization of words in Japanese, this category of names is becoming increasingly popular in Japan. Other names that cross English and Japanese phonetic boundaries are Emily (Emeri), Anna (Ana), Sara (Sara), and Marissa (Marisa).

While Emma's name has the same pronunciation in both languages, the difference lies in the English and Japanese Roman spellings (see Table 5.1). In addition, although written representations in *hiragana* and *katakana* will always be consistent, the *kanji* makeups will vary across individuals. For Emma's name, the first *kanji* is pronounced "E" and means "picture." The second *kanji*, "ma," means "dancing." Together, the *kanji* for "Emma"

Table 5.1 The orthographies and written forms of Emma's name in Japanese and English.

English, Roman	Japanese, *hiragana*	Japanese, *katakana*	Japanese, Roman	Japanese, *kanji*
(3 years, 4 months)	(4 years, 3 months)	(5 years, 2 months)	(6 years, 5 months)	(7 years, 8 months)

means "dancing picture." The choice of *kanji* depends on many different factors but is a careful decision on the part of the family.

Table 5.1 illustrates the sequential appearance of Emma's name in Japanese and English. As we can see from the dates in parentheses, Emma's initial attempt at her name was with the Roman script and the English orthography. As I presented earlier, before Emma wrote her name conventionally, she demonstrated other types of early name-writing behaviors, such as identifying and writing her name based on the first letter "E."

Hiragana followed a year after the English representation of her name, and *katakana* a year after. While Emma wrote the first three examples at home, she wrote the last two in Japanese school. By the time Emma was 6 years, 5 months old, she recognized that the Japanese Romanization of her name had a different spelling than the English version. Emma felt that this particular representation of her name was only fit for Japanese school as it did not appear anywhere else in her writing. Furthermore, Emma rarely wrote the Japanese Romanization of her name alone. It was either proceeded with or followed by the English, Roman or the Japanese *hiragana* versions. Emma wrote her name in *kanji* a year later. Jay began teaching Emma how to write her name in *kanji* when she was 6 years old. By the time Emma was 7 years old, she was learning the *kanji* for her name in Japanese school. Once she felt comfortable writing her name in *kanji*, it appeared on her Japanese schoolwork.

Taking a Curious Stance on Names

Just as Emma was at times frustrated with recreating the attributes for the written forms for her name, she possessed a curiosity about the relationship between her name and her national background. Initially, this curiosity emerged out of the idea that language generates particular national identities. For instance, back in Chapter 2, I mentioned that when Emma was 5 years, 5 months old, she asked me, "If I was born in the Year of the Tiger, why do I speak English?" Living in the USA, Emma's comments suggest that she positioned herself as an outsider. Because she was born in Japan, Emma could not understand from where the ability to speak English emerged, and she did not necessarily see herself living a bilingual life.

Not soon after, Emma (5 years, 5 months old) reproached having a Japanese name. Emma was drawing a picture of a cat and asked my opinion on what she should name it. I suggested, "Neko-cyan," whose closest English equivalent is "Ms. Kitty." Emma became upset and said, "I want an English name." Explaining that we are a Japanese- and English-speaking family was not enough for Emma, who was determined to fit into what she viewed as an English-dominant society by using an English name.

Similar to Emma's ability to regularly reproduce the graphic forms of her name, Emma was in constant upheaval on what her name meant in relation to her identity. A month after the cat-naming incident, Emma (5 years, 6 months) wrote her name in *hiragana* to a Japanese-speaking friend because she said that she "speaks both English and Japanese."

When Emma was 5 years, 8 months old, she made the declaration that she did not like her name and wanted to know why we named her Emma. I replied that we named her Emma because "it is both a Japanese and English name." Emma was a little skeptical and said, "How can that be. There are two Emmas on my bus" (there was another "Emma" who was monolingual on her bus). I took out a piece of paper and wrote her name in the English, Roman version and then in the Japanese, *hiragana* form. I explained that both representations are pronounced "Emma," although they have different scripts.

Emma seemed to accept this explanation. Two days later, Emma initiated the following dialogue.

Emma said, "I know why you named me Emma."

"And why is that?" I asked.

Emma replied, "It's a Japanese name, and if you're Japanese you need a Japanese name and that is your name. Because Emma and Ema (using the Japanese pronunciation) sound kind of the same in English and Japanese. But this is America and you speak English in America. So I guess my name is OK."

These small shifts in Emma's views about her name indicate her recognition in the possibilities that her name can play within her life. While Emma's name represents a Japanese national identity, it also aligns herself with what she viewed as important in living in the USA: the ability to speak English.

Selection of Scripts

Name writing provided Emma with an important venue to work out tensions in how she viewed herself in relation to social networks (friends, family, and community) and language practices (English and Japanese). At the realization that particular graphic forms carry meanings, Emma became conscious of which scripts she tactically employed. Her selection of scripts to write her own name provides insights into the complex relationships that existed as she lived a bicultural, bilingual, and biliterate life. Take Figure 5.5 for instance. Emma (4 years, 3 months) wrote this sign the same month in which she received the *Shimajiro* issue on *hiragana*. Emma wrote top to bottom and from right to left: "Emma," "Rika," and "Mimirin." By writing in *hiragana*, Emma created a symbolic connection between herself as a Japanese writer, her Japanese-speaking friend and Japanese pop culture. Unlike Figure 5.1, in which Emma wrote to a monolingual English-speaking individual, Emma gave this sample to me. Emma had a particular purpose: she wanted to show me her Japanese writing ability because she knew that I valued it. Through these types of experiences, Emma learned that the careful selection of scripts would win appraisal from her audience, which, in turn, would give her social and linguistic leverage. In other words, scripts provided an added benefit to her writing that could penetrate social structures (Bourdieu, 1991).

The more Emma began to understand how writing could negotiate the multiple identities, the more scripts began to emerge alongside each other. Figure 5.6 is an example. Emma (6 years, 8 months) wrote this card for my birthday. By using multiple scripts, Emma helped to define the ways in

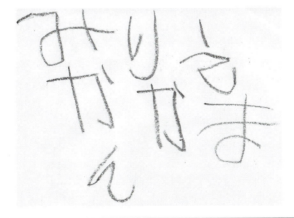

Figure 5.5 Emma (4 years, 3 months) wrote in *hiragana* (from right to left, top to bottom) "Emma," "Rika," and "Mimirin."

Figure 5.6 Emma (7 years, 5 months) wrote a birthday card for me.

which multiple languages were property, or a weighty characteristic, of our family.

The properties of any social structure, with its valued language preferences and internal organization of writing, played a major influence in how Emma wrote. In Figure 5.7, Emma (7 years, 5 months) wrote "Kabuto" in *kanji* and "Emma" in *katakana* on her Japanese work. Finding this behavior surprising, I asked Emma as to why she wrote her name in *katakana*, which is used for foreign names. Emma said, "Because I think that my name is more of an English name than a Japanese name." Emma used *katakana* to place herself outside of a Japanese school context. While her surname could be written in *kanji*, she viewed writing her given name in *katakana* as a balancing mechanism. In this way, Emma authored herself through her name-writing experiences by selecting scripts that communicated specific social and cultural meanings (Holland et al., 1998; Ivanic, 1988). In many ways, scripts were loaded

Figure 5.7 Emma (7 years, 5 months) wrote "Kabuto" in *kanji* and "Emma" in *katakana* on her Japanese schoolwork.

with significance, and Emma had control in choosing scripts that could paint portraits of herself as a bilingual and biliterate child within particular social contexts.

Script Switching

Script switching is the ability to use scripts for meaningful purposes; it is a way in which writers can blend language forms to synchronize voices to create meaningful representations. Like code switching, script switching should be seen as a natural part of a biliterate identity. It is a strategic tool used by bilingual writers, like Emma, to communicate sociocultural meanings and to foster relationships with other people and social networks. I will argue that script switching is a complex act that involves a multifaceted relationship between language structures, individuals, audience, and social and cultural contexts.

One of the earliest examples of Emma's script switching is in Figure 5.8. Emma's grandmother sent Emma origami paper from Japan, and Emma enjoyed folding the paper into various shapes, such as cats, boats, and flowers. In order to organize her origami shapes, I suggested to Emma that she make a book. Emma glued an origami shape to a piece of paper and stapled the stack of paper together. On the front of the book, Emma (4 years, 9 months) wrote "Emma's Origami." While she knew how to write her name in *hiragana* by the time she created the book, Emma wrote her name in the English, Roman version followed by "origami" in Japanese. One of the factors that may have influenced Emma's choice of scripts has to do with the grammatical structure of the language in which she was writing. If Emma wanted to write in Japanese, she would have had to have written "Emma no origami." Emma, however, started to write "Emma's" which is an English grammatical structure, which required the "S" at the end of "Emma" that could not be represented in Japanese. The interrelationship between the internal language structure and the written

Figure 5.8 Emma (4 years, 9 months) created an origami book and titled it "Emma's Origami."

language form did not give Emma a choice to script switch in the middle of the phrase "Emma's." "Origami," however, is a Japanese word that holds a specific type of sociocultural connotation that could be best represented in *hiragana*. The movement between "Emma's" and "origami" provided her the opportunity to shift from English to Japanese. Writing "origami" in *hiragana* served Emma's purposes as a writer; in fact, Emma most likely did not realize that she could write the word in English.

Another example of the influence of language structure on script switching comes from a 5-year-old Farsi-, Hebrew-, and English-speaking child, Sarah. Sarah attended a private Jewish school, called the Yeshiva, with a dual-language curriculum in English and Hebrew (Farsi was the home language). Each week, students at the Yeshiva had a bible story, or the *Parsha*. One day, after having read a story called *Vaykel*, Sarah wrote the following sentence, "The Parsha is Vaykel" as "Th PARωℵ IS VYKL" (see Figure 5.9). Sarah was able to write the first three letters of "Parsha"; however, when she came to the /sh/, she was a little unsure of the letters that made up the English diagraph. This did not deter Sarah, because in Hebrew there is a common symbol that makes that sound, ω. Sarah finished the word with the Hebrew "A," ℵ.

Sarah's script switching in this example parallels Emma's in a couple of ways. First, the written language structure influenced how and where Sarah was able to switch. Because English and Hebrew are both alphabetic languages, it was possible to represent individual sounds in both scripts. Emma could not switch when she wanted to write "Emma's" because Japanese's syllabic base does not carry a sound that represents a single "S," which forced Emma to switch between words instead of sounds.

In addition, Emma's and Sarah's script-switching examples exemplify the influences of social practices. While Emma's switch to *hiragana* demonstrated her ability to represent sociocultural knowledge, Sarah was able

Figure 5.9 Sarah (5 years) wrote "The Parsha is Vaykel" in both the English and Hebrew written forms.

to replicate the written languages that defined her school's social structure. Because *Parsha* is a Hebrew word that she learned in her dual-language school, Sarah has seen the word written in Hebrew and English. Therefore, Sarah may have thought that it was acceptable to include both forms. In other words, *Parsha* became a word that did not fit only a Hebrew or an English form; instead, it crossed written language boundaries.

Individual and Audience

Figure 5.10 illustrates how script switching allowed Emma to address multiple language audiences. Emma (7 years, 11 months) created a "family flower," which was her version of a family tree. Each petal of the flower indicated a family member. Starting at the top and moving clockwise, Emma wrote "Daddy, Obaajan [Japanese grandmother], Ojiijan [Japanese grandfather], Granddad, Auntie, Rick, Grandmom, and Mom." When I asked Emma why she decided to write Obaajan and Ojiijan in Japanese, she replied, "Because Obaajan and Ojiijan don't speak English, so I have to write in Japanese so they know what I am writing."

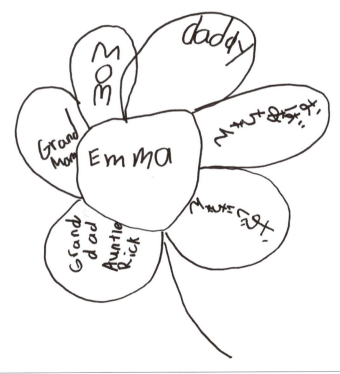

Figure 5.10 Emma (7 years, 11 months) created a family flower and wrote *Obaajan* and *Ojiijan* in *hiragana*.

In this example, Emma's main concern was making her sign under-
standable to those who her sign was about. The result was the inclusion of
two scripts. Emma could have written *Obaajan* and *Ojiijan* in the Roman
alphabet, since it is a script that is incorporated in Japanese. The inclusion
of *hiragana* held more expressive abilities for aligning the sign to two
language groups. Writing in the Roman alphabet would have done little
to show Emma's biliteracy and her connection to her Japanese family.
Writing in *hiragana*, on the other hand, was about the connection between
Emma and her audience.

This concept is illustrated in Figure 5.11. In Figure 5.11, Emma (5 years
old) created a baseball sign for Hideki Matsui. Jay was an avid Matsui fan
and watched the New York Yankees regularly on television and went to
see them at Yankee Stadium. Emma quickly became interested in Matsui.
During a mid-season slump, Jay showed disappointment at Matsui's
no-hitter game. Having seen Matsui's fans on television holding signs,
Emma decided to make a sign of her own. Emma came to me with paper
and wanted to know how to write Matsui's surname in *kanji*. I, instead,
suggested that she write it in *hiragana*. Emma became upset and said
that she needed "to write it in *kanji*." Since I did not know Matsui's *kanji*,

Figure 5.11 Emma (5 years) wrote a baseball sign for Hideki Matsui.

I suggested that she ask Jay. Jay guided Emma's hand to write the first *kanji* (*matsu*). Jay wrote the second *kanji* (*i*) on another sheet of paper and encouraged Emma to write it on her own, which she did underneath *matsu* in the middle of the paper. Once Emma wrote Matsui's name, she wrote "ganbare" ("let's go") vertically in *hiragana* on her own and wrote his number 55 on the four corners. Emma finished her sign with flowers and baseballs.

Script switching in this example occurs between *hiragana* and *kanji*. In creating the sign, Emma considered her audience, which fueled her desire to write in *kanji*. Including English did not seem to be a possibility for Emma. The reason for this conclusion is that Emma did not view Matsui as a bilingual or biliterate individual at the time. When she watched post-game shows, Matsui was always interviewed with a translator, which caused Emma to make the comment that Matsui "doesn't understand English." The extent to whether this observation was true or not is not as critical as the idea that Emma viewed Matsui as a Japanese-dominant individual. Weighing the importance of scripts in communicating meaning, Emma decided to forgo English for Japanese. At the same time, while Matsui was the person to whom the sign was directed, Emma was also writing for a larger audience: Japanese fans in the stadium. Emma's attempt to write in Japanese was a means not only for addressing Matsui but also for her to align herself with his fan base.

Social Context

There were times when the social context influenced Emma's decisions on written language within her signs. Figure 5.12 is an example. Emma's friend Erika invited Emma (5 years, 6 months) to her birthday party, which happened to be on Valentine's Day. Emma wanted to make a card for Erika, who was in Emma's class in Japanese school. Because Erika's birthday party was on Valentine's Day, Emma wrote "Happy Valentine's Day," which I spelled for her. Emma then wrote, "Erika, From Emma" in *hiragana*.

In this example, rather than writing "Happy Birthday" in Japanese, Emma considered the social holiday as part of the card. To Emma, Valentine's Day was a time when children exchanged cards, wrote notes to each other, gave small presents, and passed out candy. Most likely, from Emma's perspective, it was a special treat to have your birthday on Valentine's Day. In Japan, Valentine's Day is not considered a child's celebration. Instead, it is geared toward young couples, who have private dinners and participate in other types of special activities. In addition, Valentine's Day is the girl's responsibility in which the girl organizes activities or gives her significant other candy or gifts. Never being exposed to this interpretation

Figure 5.12 Emma (5 years, 6 months) created a birthday card for her friend Erika.

of Valentine's Day, Emma naturally saw it through an American perspective, and writing in English was the best way to represent her perception of what Valentine's Day should mean.

At the same time, while the social context encouraged Emma in one direction, she still needed to write for an audience. Erika was a Japanese-dominant child living in the USA and attending public school and Japanese school in the same district as Emma. The Japanese represents not only Erika and Emma's connection to Japanese school but also acknowledges Erika's Japanese-speaking background. This sign shows the many factors that go into play when creating signs. Decisions on how to write or represent through scripts are thoughtful and meaningful and epitomize complex relationships between individual, cultural setting, and social context.

To Switch or Not to Switch

So what are the benefits of writing in multiple languages? What drove Emma to write in multiple languages? And how did this create or recreate particular identities? Writing in multiple written languages and social life are tied in compelling ways. Emma used written language to build sets of social relationships by making sense of unfolding interactions with other people. As Emma used Japanese and English to write her name alongside other names, create cards, or label objects, she created a space where she learned something about herself. This space was not always accessible to or included adults such as myself because it was an arena where Emma could take control of how she wanted to present herself by making decisions about the local use of written language forms through the selection of scripts.

Switching as a Linguistic Tool

Script switching in real-life writing situations was a linguistic tool for accomplishing a goal. As Emma and Sarah have shown us, children select scripts that help them move out of states of disequilibrium. Knowing that "Emma's" is not a grammatical, phonetic, or orthographic feature of Japanese, Emma accommodated her current linguistic knowledge by writing in two scripts. By doing so, Emma demonstrated emergent linguistic knowledge of Japanese and English that framed and influenced how she wrote. Sarah provided another example of how she easily moved between writing features. In fact, although Sarah and Emma were not able to articulate the reasons behind their actions, the extent of their knowledge in their respective languages is clearly evident. These observations and conclusion confirm how bilingual and biliterate children are cognitively and linguistically flexible when language is recognized as a resource in emergent biliteracy.

Martinez-Roldan and Sayer argue, "Bilinguals have special linguistic resources beyond what monolinguals in either of the languages have, and [they] are able to employ these resources strategically and with great sensitivity to contextual factors" (2006: 296). Emma supports Martinez-Roldan and Sayer's argument that bilingual children are strategic in their written-language use. Like code switching, script switching as a linguistic tool uncovered the potential that Emma held in her ability to process linguistic knowledge across written language systems. Instead of situating written language as language separation, Emma saw it as a blending of language forms that could be implemented tactically to communicate meaning.

Furthermore, script switching illustrates Emma's linguistic competence. There are several takes on linguistic competence. Noam Chomsky was renowned for his work on the Language Acquisition Device (LAD). Chomsky concluded that humans have an innate ability to learn grammar, which is the result of the LAD. According to Chomsky, linguistic competence is the ability to generate a boundless number of grammatical structures within sentences. Emma and Sarah have shown a new perspective on linguistic competence from this perspective. Emma possessed a certain degree of fluidity in moving between the internal structures of

Japanese and English. By doing so, she developed competence as she became metacognitive about the similarities and differences in linguistic structures. Although Emma and Sarah produced writing that was visually different from writing in one script, in neither example did they disrupt the grammatical or organizational structure of their respective languages.

In fact, by supplementing one writing feature for another—one alphabet for another to represent a sound or group of sounds, for example—both Emma and Sarah cultivated their underlying proficiency in both languages (Cummins, 1984). Consequently, Emma and Sarah could work in cognitively demanding situations. For instance, the fact that Sarah was able to complement the English diagraph /sh/ with the Hebrew {ω} does not inhibit her developing writing proficiency. Instead, Sarah's actions allowed her to work through the unknown. She efficiently transferred one form of knowledge to another allowing her to overcome cognitive challenges.

Switching as a Social Tool

While Chomsky proposed that linguistic competence is strictly reduced to the individual speaker's ability to produce language, other researchers have argued that this perspective of language falls short of describing practical language embedded within social contexts (Thompson, quoted in Bourdieu, 1991). Bourdieu (1991) suggests that there is a practical competence in which an individual can produce language that is appropriate for the circumstances. As Thompson describes, "Their practical competence involves not only the capacity to produce grammatical utterances, but also the capacity to make oneself heard, believed, obeyed, and so on" (quoted in Bourdieu, 1991: 8).

Script switching was a way by which Emma could address a wider linguistic audience. In order to do so, she needed to assess the expressive capacities of the available scripts and the conditions by which her sign would be received and valued by her audience (Bourdieu, 1991). Emma measured the possible receptions that she would receive by considering her audience's language preference, the social context, and the meaning she wanted to convey. Emma's family flower is a good example. Directing her flower to her Japanese grandparents and to those in her family who do not speak Japanese, Emma used two scripts that would appropriately express her family structure.

Therefore, Emma's signs were not only a reflection of herself, they were also an appraisal of the addressee's voice (Holquist, 1981). This constant consideration of how her signs would be received caused Emma to accordingly adjust the scripts she employed in anticipation of the response that she thought she would receive.

At the same time, while script switching was a social tool for Emma to communicate with her audience, it was also a tool to align to or to challenge the social structures within which her signs were embedded. Emma's name writing exemplified this point. Any writing is embedded with some type of social structure (i.e. home, school, company, etc.). Emma's writing her name in Japanese school illustrates how social structures have properties that will value or devalue certain writing features. While Romanization of Japanese words is a plausible way to write, it is not valued as much as writing the other three scripts within Japanese school. Recognizing that certain scripts are weighed more than others, Emma appeared to prefer writing her name in *hiragana*, *katakana*, and *kanji*. Emma possessed what Bourdieu (1991) termed linguistic capital. Linguistic capital within an early biliteracy framework refers to one's ability to produce written language forms appropriate for particular social structures. In turn, the social structure values the written language form and the individual producing it. When Emma exhibited pieces of her developing linguistic capital, she aligned herself with the social structure and others participating within it.

Alignment, however, is not always the result. For instance, Emma wrote in *katakana* in Japanese school because she identified herself with both Japanese and American society. Because writing in the Roman alphabet would not have developed her linguistic capital, the next best step would be to write in *katakana*. Writing in *katakana*, while it showed her ability to apply her writing to certain properties of Japanese school, also challenged other aspects of the social structure. Writing her name in *katakana*, Emma positioned herself as a "foreigner" who could challenge the exclusiveness of Japanese within its structure. In essence, the selection of *katakana*, at the time, provided Emma her access but also gave her a means for expressing how she could identify herself as a biliterate child growing up in a bilingual home in American society. These identities were not established ways of acting and reacting. Instead, they were fluid. Emma forwent *katakana* for *kanji*, which represented the highest type of linguistic capital, as she progressed through school.

As Emma became older, she was better able to anticipate how writing forms were a means for developing sets of social relationships and access into different social structures. Emma's signs were sites of negotiation and contemplation about who she was, who others were around her, and the meaning of writing and communication. Coming full circle, her signs were places of discovery. Not only did Emma learn about the forms and functions of writing and drawing that developed her linguistic competence. She also discovered that writing provided her with a certain degree of power, liberation, and negotiation in expressing her identities as she aligned with and challenged social structures. This practical competence fed into a pool of developing linguistic capital.

Summary

Writing in English and Japanese afforded Emma many benefits. Emma's writing highlights how writing development is not exclusively tied to linguistic competence, it also includes developing a practical ability to appropriate language for the audience and social context. Naturally the social context framed the ways in which language was used. But forsaking social abilities for linguistic superiority can minimize the complexity to which Emma approximated written language forms in meaningful social contexts, which are equally important in developing biliterate proficiency. As a result, writing in English and Japanese allowed Emma to work through states of disequilibrium, express knowledge that is not always translatable in other languages, and to address a more extensive network of language preferences.

At the same time, writing in English and Japanese involved learning to be someone in a complicated world defined by language variables, social structures, and valued forms of writing. In order to grow as a young biliterate child, Emma had to assess the benefits and limitations of scripts in relation to the social structures within which they were embedded and how they will be valued. As Emma engaged in this active exploration, she negotiated the ways that she could portray who she was, or her sense of self. In this way, writing in multiple languages reproduces or challenges particular social identities.

Reaction Questions

As a classroom teacher, what would you do if you heard Emma say that she wanted an English name instead of a Japanese name? What if you heard another child inquire to the origins of Emma's name?

Suggested Activities

1. Have children investigate the origins of their names.
2. Find "experts" in other languages. Ask them to write your students' names in their expert language. Talk about the similarities and differences in their given names and their names in the other languages.
3. Observe an early biliterate child. Is there evidence of script switching? If so, when and where does the child script switch? What are the purposes of the script switch?

CHAPTER **6**

Reading as Social Practice

Breaking the Code of Code Switching

Like writing, reading has a strong social foundation. To illustrate, consider the following dialogue between Emma and myself.

"Why is Silly Sally so silly?" Emma (5 years, 1 month) asked.

"Why do you think that she is silly?" I returned.

"I don't know. You always read the book to me," Emma countered as she flipped through the pages of the book.

"Why don't you try to read the book so you can figure out why Sally is so silly?" I questioned.

Emma opened up the book and began to read: "Silly Sally went to town walking backwards upside down. On her pig, she met a pig, a silly pig, they danced a jig. Silly Sally went to town walking backwards upside down."

Emma continued to read to page 16. She then read, "On the way she met a sheep. A silly sheep, they slept. But how could Sally get to town while she's sleeping? On her way she took Neddy Buttercup with her."

"That's why Sally is so silly! You can't walk when you're sleeping and upside down!" Emma suddenly replied. She continued to read, "He tickled the pig who danced the jig."

Just as Emma wrote relationships with other people, the dialogue provides a window into the ways in which her oral reading of *Silly Sally* (Wood, 1994) emerged out of our social interactions. Having heard the book many times, Emma raised a question about the text to which I chose not to respond directly. Instead, I encouraged Emma to read the text to find the answer to her question. Although I knew that she was not an independent reader, I valued the sense that she could make from the text if she attempted to read it herself.

In fact, Emma employed a variety of strategies to create a parallel text that matched the story structure and illustrations to predict upcoming sequences (Goodman, 1996). This point is illustrated when she first encountered the phrase "on the way she met a pig," which she read as "on her pig." Emma most likely thought that the text should read "on her way." As she balanced the story structure with the pictures, she realized that the word "pig" should appear as it is the sole image on the page. The interactions between the story structure and the illustrations caused Emma to read an ungrammatical word sequence, which she did not, at this point, disconfirm. But Emma did not keep this structure throughout her reading. Instead, by the time she reached page 16, Emma had worked out the structure and read the expected phrase.

Emma's oral reading demonstrates her early proficient reading. Early proficient readers are early readers who create parallel texts that correspond to the illustrations and story structure over the graphic cues (Goodman et al., 2007). Emma fell into early proficient reading behaviors when she left the rhyme and repetition to create a text that made sense and aligned itself with the illustrations. Emma read, "Now how did Sally get to town, sleeping backwards, upside down? Along came Neddy Buttercup, walking forwards, right side up" as "But how could Sally get to town while she's sleeping? On her way, she took Neddy Buttercup with her."

At the same time, initiation into reading the text took place on a social plane rather than on an individual one. With my encouragement, Emma read without interference from me and appeared to answer her question as to why Sally was silly. My actions toward Emma's reading helped in constructing her sense of self as a reader. I gave her permission to attempt the text on her own and accepted her reading by privileging her invented reading over accuracy. Emma's reading had a purpose over and beyond orally reading the texts for assessment and documentation reasons. The reading event was authentic; it was embedded within a social context and developed around interpersonal relationships between two people who had a vested interest in and particular views of reading.

This chapter will delve deeper into reading as social practice with the focus on connecting reading to both linguistic strategies and social ways of negotiating reading events. The beginning of the chapter will examine how reading for Emma was a social act that unfolded as Jay and I co-constructed reading formats and participation patterns through a code-switching framework. The second half of the chapter will connect the linguistic and social dimensions of reading to better understanding how reading evolves out of the way we positioned Emma as a reader.

Reading as Social and Verbal Acts

When Emma was 10 years old, I asked her if she remembered how she learned to read.

"Do you remember how you learned to read?" I asked.

"I started with my letter-sounds and then I put them together," Emma replied.

"Is there anything else?" I questioned.

"It was so long ago. If I remember anything else, I'll let you know," Emma said.

Emma's memory of learning to read does not coincide with how she actually approached beginning reading. Emma described her process as a technical skill in which she had to know the letter-sounds that she needed to put together to form words. In fact, her description sounds more like the discourse that is used in talking about reading in schools rather than the way in which it naturally occurred in the home as seen in the above dialogue.

Ways with Printed Words

For Emma, not only was early reading a socially constructed act between family members, it was also critical for linguistic stimulation. In particular, reading and interacting around reading with Emma created initial steps toward helping her develop an awareness of others, her family, herself, and print (Tabors & Snow, 2002). The following dialogue illustrates this point. Emma (6 years, 5 months) was reading an excerpt from a storybook *Shimajiro* (2005). Jay was trying to help Emma read and answer a series of word plays presented in the text. In the following dialogue, Emma attempted to read the word play, "San to ichi ga haite iru tabemono wa nani? [What food has a *san* ("three") and *ichi* ("one") in it?]" (*Shimajiro*, 2005: 15). After Emma read the word play, she needed to draw a line to the answer *sandoiichi*, or sandwich.

"Tugi. Nan-tte kaite aru?" Jay told Emma to move to the next word play and asked her what the word play said.

"San to ichi ta [3 and 1]," Emma read.

"Ga," Jay immediately corrected.

"Ga," Emma repeated and code switched to ask, "What's this?"

"Ha," Jay read to Emma.

"Haite ru tabemono wa nani? [What food has it in it?]" Emma finished reading.

"Sore. Nani sore? Nani kaite aru?" Jay pointed to the picture of the sandwich and asked Emma what the picture was. He then asked her to read the text.

"Sandoiichi [Sandwich]," Emma read.

"Hai," Jay said that Emma was right. "San to ichi deshita. Sen o hiite kudasai," Jay replied that "sandoiichi" has a *san* and an *ichi* and asked Emma to draw a line to the answer.

Recognizing Emma's early, independent reading behaviors, Jay modified his role and participation within the event to accommodate Emma's developing reading ability. Playing less of the reader role, he encouraged Emma to tackle the reading tasks and assisted in the oral reading. For instance, Jay corrected Emma when she read "ta" for "ga." This oral substitution disrupted the meaning and the grammatical structure of the sentence. "Ga" is a subject article, which means that it clues the reader as to the subject of the sentence. Within the question, the article indicates that the answer is a thing, or as a direct translation might read, "What is the food that has a san and an ichi?" "Ta" does not serve this function.

At the same time, these types of early exposures to reading aided in Emma's knowledge about the forms and internal structure of written languages. The text in the book is written as:

３と一がはいってるたべものはなあに？

There are three Japanese scripts used in the sentence, which is read from top to bottom and right to left (i.e. starting at the number 3 and moving down and toward the left). The number 3 is written in the Roman alphabet, while the number 1 is written in *kanji*. The rest of the question is written in *hiragana*. At the same time, the answer to the question is a Western concept, which resulted in the answer "sandwich" being written in *katakana* as サンドイチ. By reading the word play, Emma learned about Japanese reading directionality, the grammatical structure of sentences, and the organization of Japanese writing forms. The dialogue suggests that Emma moved effortlessly between these characteristics when she engaged in meaningful activities and through natural and supportive interactions with print with her father.

Jay and I were Emma's first "teachers" of reading. She began to understand print concepts, the relationships between oral and written language, and how reading works. She developed discourses around reading, such as turning the page, talking about the front and back of the book, and using book language (i.e. "Once upon a time"). Our goal was to assist Emma's ability within the event. From our standpoint, we wanted her to be an independent reader who would be able to work with Japanese and English texts. In order to do so, we employed strategies that would take us to that goal.

Parents as Strategic Partners

Jay and I were rarely passive bystanders when Emma attempted to read. This theme came out when listening to the transcripts over the four years of documenting Emma's biliteracy. There was always a comment or two and an invitation from Emma to join in the reading. As the two scenarios presented thus far show, we, as parents, always had the freedom of deciding when and how to participate. Gee (2005) describes these types of inter-actions between "newbies" (Emma) and "masters" (Jay and I) as a way for participants to enter the same space to complete common endeavors. In doing so, Jay and I employed strategies in order to address the purpose of the activity, Emma's ability, and the choices made by Emma.

The majority of the reading events were the result of Jay, Emma, and I creating a dialogic context (Whitehurst in Bus, 2002) in which all mem-bers listened to, questioned, and prompted each other to create an inquiry situation that allowed for entrance into and engagement with the text. To illustrate, consider the following dialogue in which Emma (6 years and 6 months) and Jay were completing a word maze in an activity book (*Popikko Doriru*, n.d.). The word maze required the reader to fill in a new word with the last syllable of the previous word. For instance, the word "apple," *ringo*, ends with *-go*. The next word in the maze must start with *go-*, such as the word *gomibako*, which means "trash can."

"Shiteru desyo?" Jay said that Emma should know what it is, "Ki," Jay continued by giving Emma a hint.

"Kitune," Emma replied.

"Kitune. Ne," Jay led Emma to the next word.

"Nekutai," Emma said.

"Hai," Jay responded that Emma was right, "I ga tuite iru?" Jay ques-tioned Emma by asking her what word starts with an "I."

"Isu," Emma answered.

"Kore wa," Jay asked about the object in the picture.

"Sushi," Emma said, "Dadi no suki na sushi." Emma commented that sushi was her dad's favorite food.

"Hai. Tugi wa?" Jay agreed and asked Emma what would come next.

"Shi . . . shi . . . shirani," Emma repeated the last syllable *-shi* and then said that she did not know.

Jay repeated, "Shirani?"

"Shirani," Emma said that she did not know, "Shika." Emma quickly added the next word, "deer."

The dialogue illustrates the ways in which Emma and Jay were listening and responding to each other's conversational moves. In the opening of the dialogue, Jay prompted Emma by giving her a hint and suggesting that she knew the next word in the maze. Emma followed Jay's question with an immediate response to the next word in the maze. Jay listened to Emma's response and tried to be one step ahead of her by giving her a clue to the next word.

Instead of immediately providing the answer, Jay constructed a context by prompting Emma with a variety of clues. While there were times when Jay provided Emma with the beginning sound of the next word, he also pointed to pictures of upcoming words. For instance, when the next word needed to start with *su*-, Jay pointed to the picture of sushi rather than giving the initial *su*- sound.

However, Emma ran into some trouble when she could not figure out the next word. Emma repeated the -*shi* sound and then said that she did not know. Rather than immediately providing Emma with the answer, Jay questioned her by saying, "You don't know?" Emma confirmed that she did not know but quickly came up with the next word. By listening to Emma, Jay's conversational maneuvers show how he was selective in how and when he wanted to participate. Being embedded within a parent–child dynamic provided Jay with more freedom in modifying his participation than Emma. For instance, Jay tried to guide Emma back into the activity by saying, "Next" when he felt that Emma was getting off-task when she commented that her father liked sushi.

Jay's control does not necessarily mean that Emma had a complete lack of control. There was constant negotiation occurring between members as each positioned the other in different roles. The creation of particular types of participation structures, or an interaction pattern between the participants, in reading events in both Japanese and English texts resulted from these negotiations (Gregory, 1996). In other words, Jay and I used social strategies to move Emma's engagement and reading ability forward. These strategies developed and fed into larger participation structures between family members. Before discussing the ways in which shifts in participation structures were also a shift in identity, I will discuss the different strategies that Jay and I used when reading with Emma.

Asking Questions

Jay and I raised questions to allow Emma to predict upcoming texts. For instance, in the following dialogue, Emma (5 years, 10 months) read *Kasa* (Matsuno, 1985) to her father.

Emma read page 18: "Kuroi kasa. Dare no kasa. [The black umbrella. Whose is it?]"

Jay said he wondered whose umbrella it could be by asking, "Dare no ka naa?"

Emma turned the page and read, "Ookii kasa! Otoosan no? [It's a big umbrella! Is it Father's?]"

Jay confirmed that it belonged to the father, "Otoosan no nee."

Within this snippet of dialogue, Emma was engaged in reading the text and Jay participated alongside Emma by raising questions based on Emma's reading. The picture on page 18 showed a person behind a black umbrella with black rainboots. The illustrator does not show the person's face on page 19 or 21. When Emma read, "The black umbrella. Whose is it?" Jay questioned, "Whose umbrella could it be?" Jay's question sounds like a think-aloud or a verbal prediction that he placed on interpersonal plane. The text on the next page does not necessarily answer the question as it read, "It's a big umbrella! Is it Father's?" Jay, however, answered his prediction by saying that it belonged to the father. Jay modeled how a reader predicts upcoming ideas and text even though he never directly addressed Emma.

There were similar situations with Emma and me when reading English text. In the following Emma (6 years, 2 months) read *I Went Walking* (Williams, 1989).

Emma started to read on page 14: "I went walking. What do you see? I saw a green duck looking at me. I went walking."

"What do you think it's going to be?" I asked.

"It's going to be a pig," Emma replied and turned the page. "I knew it," she said.

She continued reading, "I saw a pink pig looking at me."

The illustration on the page with the text "What did you see?" shows the back end of the animal that will appear on the following page. After reading "I saw a green duck looking at me," she read the next page, "I went walking." I immediately jumped in with a predictive question, "What do you think it's going to be?" This question actually rephrased the text, "What did you see?" Emma recognized that I was not reading the text and answered my question by looking in the bottom-right corner for the part of the animal that would appear. When Emma turned the page, she confirmed her prediction and read the text.

In addition, while I chimed in to focus Emma on meaning, I did not do so when it came to accuracy. Emma read "What did you see?" as "What do you see?" throughout the entire text. Because I felt that Emma's sentence made sense, I did not see the necessity in interfering with her reading. In part, this has to do with my beliefs on how reading should be defined. If I thought accuracy was important, I may have corrected Emma, but accuracy was not my immediate goal for her.

Rephrasing Texts

Another common strategy that Jay and I used was rephrasing texts, or labeling and describing events or things in the story. This is a well-noted strategy used by parents when reading with their children (Laakso in Bus, 2002). To provide an example from Emma and Jay's interactions with *Kasa*, Jay rephrased Emma's oral reading in the following dialogue.

Emma read on page 16, "Kasa sashite kaerou? [Should we put up our umbrellas and go home?]"

"Kasa sashite karou nee. Ame fute kita nee," Jay rephrased the question in the text and said, "That's right. Let's put up the umbrella and go home. It started to rain."

Emma continued to read, "Kuroi kasa. Dare no kasa? [The black umbrella. Whose is it?]"

In this instance, Jay took the question that was presented in the text and put it into a declarative. He followed the sentence with a reason as to why the character should use the umbrella—it started to rain—which was shown in the illustrations. Emma did not directly acknowledge Jay's entrance into the text, which suggests that Jay's talk appeared as a side bar of conversation that rhythmically kept the shared reading intact. In other words, Jay's rephrasing confirmed what Emma orally read.

In another instance, I also rephrased Emma's oral reading, but for a slightly different purpose. In the following example, Emma (6 years, 5 months) read *Dear Zoo* (Campbell, 1982).

She read, "And sent me a puppy. He was pet. I keeped him. The End."

"They sent him a puppy. He was perfect. He kept him. The End," I said.

This example illustrates how I reformed the ungrammatical sentence to the expected sentences. These verbal interactions created a shared frame of reference between Emma and us. We were talking about and discussing the texts while verbalizing strategies that modeled predicting, confirming, and correcting approaches to reading (Goodman, 1996). In turn, these approaches became shared knowledge between participants.

Acceptance of Code-Switching Behaviors

Code switching was a common behavior in Emma's oral language when reading text, particularly when reading Japanese texts. In the following dialogue, Emma (5 years, 10 months) and Jay read a Japanese book *Ushiro ni iru no dare* (Fukuda, 2003).

Emma read, "Neko chyan. [The cat.]"

"Neko san," Jay corrected with the emphasis on "san."

"San?" Emma code switched, "I thought it was *chyan*."

"Neko san no ushiro ni iru no dare," Emma continued to read.

Emma read "the cat" as *neko-chyan* instead of *neko-san*. While Emma's attempt made sense and still meant "cat," the difference in the two versions lay in the *chyan* and *san*. *Chyan* is used as a suffix to identify young girls or female animals (*kun* is used for the male counterpart). An adult, on the other hand, would take the suffix *san*. Emma, at the age of 5, was called "Emma chyan" rather than "Emma san." Emma mostly likely predicted *chyan* because she hears this suffix most often and the illustrations show a small, cute cat. When Jay corrected Emma, she repeated *san* and then said in English, "I thought it was *chyan*." This code switch represents a grammatical, or complex, code switch, which means that Emma switched languages as indicated by a switch in grammar. There is another code switch also present. In the sentence "I thought it was *chyan*," Emma made a one-word code switch. Sociolinguists suggest that while there are two major types of code switches, grammatical and one-word, they argue that grammatical code switches are "true switches" (Auer, 1999b; Reyes, 2004; Romaine, 1995).

While this may be the case, one-word switches did serve meaningful purposes for Emma. There were times when Emma may not have known a word in either Japanese or English. This effective strategy allowed her to focus on communication; she could keep her thoughts going and express the big ideas within her conversation. As in Emma's example above, certain words cannot be readily translated because they hold particular socio-cultural meanings. A direct translation of *chyan* does not exist, and the closest equivalency would be "Miss." "Miss," however, is used for an unmarried female, generally, under the age of 18. It is not customary to use "Miss" when referring to animals. Emma's use of *chyan* was a better choice to represent sociocultural knowledge.

Like in her writing, Jay and I tended to accept Emma's code switching. I, however, never observed Emma switching when working with English texts. There could be many reasons for this observation. I am inclined to believe that the effects of living in an English-dominant community and attending a school that privileged English over other languages played an important role in her language preferences. She probably felt Japanese texts and aspects of the language more challenging, which gave rise to code switching. For instance, Emma code switched above to question the text. In order to do so, she needed to move out of the text, which was in Japanese. Switching to English was a way in which Emma could move out of the Japanese texts to question and, as we will see later, problem solve while keeping with the goal of the activity.

In other words, code switching provided Emma with what sociolinguists call a "verbal strategy" (Auer, 1999b). In this sense, she used code switching strategically to attain both short-term conversational goals and long-term aims. For instance, bilingual speakers may code switch to negotiate power relationships or to take control of the conversation. The long-term result is that they acquire domination within that community of speakers. Thus, code switching allowed Emma to question her father and the text with the long-term goal of better understanding how reading works by making reading strategies visible.

Breaking the Code of Code Switching

Code switching served different purposes in Emma's reading ranging from trying to problem solve when she came to difficult areas to trying to verbally negotiate the reading tasks. There were also times when her code switches were text-related, meaning that the text would be in Japanese and Emma would switch to English. While Emma switched to English, she was still talking about the text. On the other hand, Emma's code switches could be participant-related (Auer, 1999a). For instance, while she was reading a text that was in Japanese, she may have code switched to speak English with another person in her immediate surroundings. This participant-related code switch involved more conversational maneuvers than reading or staying with the text.

Sequential Contrast

Sequential contrast code switches were text-related code switches that discussed the text but the language of the text and Emma's conversational language contrasted each other, such as reading a Japanese text but using English to question or comment on it. These code switches were in an immediate sequence to text. For instance, in the following example Emma (5 years, 9 months) read a storybook, *Otsukisama konbawa* (Hayashi, 1986) with me.

"Otsuki sama konbaha . . . konbaha [Good evening Moon, Good evening]," Emma read *konbaha* instead of *konbawa*.

"What does that mean?" Emma asked.

"Konbaha?" I replied.

"Konbawa!" Emma corrected.

In this instance, Emma created a nonword in Japanese by reading *konbaha*. Not recognizing the word, Emma code switched to English to question her miscue. Although I raised a question, Emma never responded to me. These types of code switches had the characteristics of egocentric talk; they did not appear to serve an immediate social function and served as a problem-solving strategy. As Vygotsky (1986) found in egocentric talk, these code switches increased as texts became more challenging or when Emma came across difficult or questionable parts.

In the following example, Emma (5 years, 10 months) read the picture book *Kasa* (Matsuno, 1985).

"Kasa sashite e [Let's put up the umbrella]," Emma read and instead of reading *ka* she read *e*.

"No," Emma immediately added, "Kasa sashite kaerou [Let's put up the umbrella and go home.]" She self-corrected herself and read the expected sentence.

Emma was predicting upcoming words when she produced *e* in *kae*. She recognized that her produced sentence did not make sense and was not graphically similar to the expected response. This caused her to code switch to English to say, "No." Once she disconfirmed her prediction, she self-corrected to the expected sentence.

In addition to using code switching to articulate the ways in which she monitored herself, Emma made text-to-text or text-to-self connections in order to make sense of what she was reading. In the following example, Emma (5 years, 5 months) had to answer a quiz question, which was, "Which one is the tallest mountain in Japan?" She needed to select from the two responses, "Ojiisan" (Uncle) and "Fijisan" (Mount Fuji) (*Shimajiro*, 2005, p. 18).

"Nihonichi takai yama no namae wa dottchi? [Which one is the tallest mountain in Japan?]" Jay read.

"Shiranai," Emma said that she did not know, "They are the same height?" Emma said about the picture which showed two mountains at the same height.

"De moo, namae?" Jay asked the names under the pictures.

"Fujisan! How tall is it? I remember that it is higher than Tokyo Tower," Emma replied.

"Mochiron. Tokyo Tower yori takai yo," Jay said of course that it is taller than Tokyo Tower.

When encountered with a problem in the above conversation, Emma was unsure of the answer to the question because the text presented two mountains the same height. Jay encouraged Emma to read the text under the illustrations, which clued Emma into the answer to the question. On the one hand, Emma knew that *ojiisan* would not make sense. On the other hand, *Fujisan* not only made better sense, but also Emma read about Fujisan in another book. After Emma selected her answer, she code switched to English to make a text-to-text connection, which in turn allowed her to make associations to her background knowledge.

Change in Mode of Interaction

Emma's code switches were also related to other people around her. Certain code switches attempted to change the mood of the interaction as she code switched to project herself in different ways (Goffman, 1981). For instance, in the following dialogue, which is part of an earlier dialogue where Emma was completing word plays, Jay asked her to draw a line from the word play to the answer in the activity book *Shimajiro* (2005).

"Erebe-ta-," Emma said that the answer to the word play was "elevator."
Jay said to Emma that she should draw a line, "Sen hiite kudasai."
Emma replied laughingly, "OK, Mister."

Emma's code switch showed herself as funny or silly. "OK, Mister" was one of her favorite phrases during this time and she often used it when she gave in to a request. Emma's code switch also signaled a little more than just projecting herself differently within the conversation. It also indicated how she used code switching in negotiating power relationships embedded within the parent–child dynamic. Jay rarely code switched when reading with Emma as seen in the conversations presented in this chapter. Emma, however, knew that her father was also a bilingual speaker. The switch in English changed the footing of the conversation where Emma had the "leg-up" rather than her father, although she did give in to Jay's request. In other words, Emma could comply but also exert a piece of her language identity and negotiate the dynamics of the social interactions.

Topic Change

Changing the topic through code switching was another way Emma used language to navigate particular requests that were placed on her (Reyes, 2004). In the following example, Jay and Emma were working the word plays in *Shimajiro* (2005). This dialogue is a continuation of the above conversation.

"Moo ikai yonde," Jay asked Emma to read the word one more time.
"Shya . . . be . . . ru. Shyaberu [Shovel]," Emma read.
"Hanasenai no ni, shyaberi shichyou, shyaberu," Jay summarized the word play as although the shovel cannot talk, it ends up saying words. The Japanese word for "shovel" is *shyaberu*, which also means "to talk."
"Can you buy me a cake? This one looks so good," Emma said pointing to the picture on the page.
"Ma-mi kitte mite," Jay said to ask me.

Within this conversation, Emma and Jay were working on the word plays, but Emma tried to change the topic of conversation away from the word plays to buying her cake. These topic changes were attempts to divert Jay's attention away from the goal; code switching was a conver-sational maneuver for Emma to try to modify and reconstruct pieces of the interaction. Furthermore, in this example, we can see how Jay accepted Emma's code switching but did not feel that he needed to modify his language within the conversation.

Setting Off

Some of Emma's participant-related code switches set off personal stories. Unlike sequential contrast code switches, these switches did not appear to have an immediate problem-solving effect with the text. In the following excerpt, Jay and Emma (5 years, 10 months) were reading a book with an octopus in the illustrations.

"Kore nani?" Pointing to the picture of the octopus, Jay asked Emma what it was called. Emma did not know and shrugged her shoulders.

"Tako da yo," Jay replied that it was an octopus.

"Tako! Tako!" Emma exclaimed. "Is that a dog?" she asked pointing to the illustration on the next page.

"Do you remember when Kady stole Ricky's cookie?" Emma asked.

"Mmmm," Jay said.

The picture of the dog on the next page triggered Emma to go off into a personal story about her grandmother's dog Kady. Comparing this code switch with a sequential contrast, setting-off code switches were ways that Emma could move out of the activity to tell a story. While the story may have been related to the text, it did not serve as an immediate problem-solving tool. In this particular dialogue, Emma was not having difficulty with some piece of the story. Instead, the text set off a memory that Emma wanted to convey, and she did so in English.

Making Second Attempts

Code switches also were ways in which Emma reformulated an utterance or the language preference of the participant (Auer, 1999a). Here, for instance, Emma (5 years, 6 months) and Jay were working on completing a *Shimajiro* activity during which Emma had to place stickers on Japan's prefectures. Emma was looking for Okinawa Prefecture, which is the most southern island of Japan.

"Koko? Atsui tokoro?" Emma asked if she should put the sticker in the space she was pointing to, which she referred to as "the hot place."

"Okinawa ken. Hikoki no shiru hareba ii zya," Jay repeated Okinawa Prefecture and told Emma to put a sticker on it. Emma did not see Jay's statement as a response to her question.

"Doko?" Emma again asked where she should put the sticker. "I don't know," Emma said.

"Okinawa ken," Jay replied pointing to the map to the small island, "kono shima."

Emma tried to make two attempts in getting information from Jay that would help her to complete the task. Afterwards, Emma code switched to English to place emphasis on her current state of uncertainty to which Jay responded and pointed out the place in question.

In my discussion with writing, I argued that script-switching was a way for Emma to write relationships with other people and to align herself with or challenge social contexts and her audience through the use of scripts. Code switching held a similar function. It was a learning tool when she came across difficulty in her reading. At the same time, it was a conversational tool as she tried to negotiate with other people around her. What I have just described is the short-term goals of code switching.

As I stated in Chapter 5, language separation did not equate with reading and writing competence for Emma. Competence has to do with social ability as much as with linguistic knowledge. Code switching allowed Emma to develop a deeper sense of not only how to work with texts but also how to employ language that would allow her to move herself forward in her reading competence. At the same time, reading was embedded within social relationships and family dynamics that Emma needed to navigate, which she also did through language. This navigation cultivated Emma's practical competence (Bourdieu, 1991).

To Switch or Not to Switch: Reading

The benefits of code switching need to be thought about in terms of short-term and long-term goals (Wei, 1999). Short-term goals related to the immediate, observable ways that she used code switching as a social and linguistic tool within conversations around texts. The long-term effects are less instant and more gradual; they happen over a period of time and through multiple interactions with language, texts, and other people.

Switching as a Linguistic and Cognitive Tool

While reading has its social roots, it is also a cognitive task. Particularly for beginning readers like Emma, the task can be daunting. Not only must Emma comprehend what she was reading but also she needed to make sense of the connections between oral and written languages when reading in either Japanese or English. Emma's ability to understand that written marks can be read heralded an important literacy milestone, and her rendition of *Silly Sally* is an example of how she understood that written language relates to oral language. But to what extent? And, from Emma's perspective, what is the best route in bridging that connection?

Looking across Emma's reading patterns as a beginning reader can provide some insights into how she began to bridge the connections between reading and oral language. Emma's early proficient reading behaviors during *Silly Sally* exemplifies how she needed story structure and patterning to guide her through the book. And they worked well for her. When they did not, she supplemented her reading with text that she created and followed how she perceived the story should flow. Emma, at the time, did not have full control over the phonology–orthography relationships in English. While Emma understood that oral language can be transformed into written language, she was still developing what characteristics of oral language would fit into the forms and internal structures of English.

The more Emma became aware of the relationships between the phonology and orthography in English, the more she became concerned with them. Instead of using holistic strategies to supplement unknown areas in the text, she honed into the graphic information. Emma, however, never gave up meaning. Her shift to the graphic information suggests the importance that she placed in supplementing graphophonic cues to support her reading. Emma's reading one year after *Silly Sally* illustrates this point.

Emma (6 years, 2 months) and I were reading *I Went Walking* (Williams, 1989). I introduced a part of this reading earlier to demonstrate how I assisted Emma in predicting upcoming text. In this episode, Emma started reading the first page of the book.

"I went calk . . . I went walking," Emma read. "I almost said 'calking,' " she said laughing.

"I went walking. Went do you . . . what do you see?" Emma continued reading. "I . . . I don't know this word," Emma said as she was trying to read "saw." Attempting the sounds in the word, Emma said, "sow a black cat."

"What does 'sow' mean?" Emma asked with a little giggle.

"What do you think that word might mean? Keep trying," I replied.

Emma tried skipping the phrase and read, "At me . . . Looking at me. I saw."

"Is it 'saw'?" she asked.

I gave her a smile, and she kept reading: "I saw a black cat looking at me. I went walking. I . . . What do you see? I saw a brown horse looking at me."

When Emma wanted to read "saw," she read it as "sow." Although "sow" is a word, it was not the word that she needed in the context because "I sow a black cat" did not make sense. This prompted her to ask me the meaning of "sow." When I did not provide her with the answer, she continued to read on, and the context of the rest of the sentence provided her with semantic information that she needed. Emma's focus on the graphic information did not take away from meaning. The attention to the surface features of English was a part of her natural progression in her reading. Emma did not need overt instruction to attend to the phonology of written language. Instead, she instructed herself as she became more aware of the organization of written language.

This integration required cognitive work on behalf of Emma for the reason that English has inconsistent relationships between phonology and orthography. Words cannot be simply "sounded out" because of the variety of influences that have shaped the English language, which was described in detail in Chapter 3. Based on social influences that framed her understanding of written and oral languages, Emma needed to make mental connections between what she heard and saw around her, which required active exploration of language in different contexts. Reading in Japanese was similar. Consider the following dialogue when Emma read *Ushiro ni iru no dare* (Fukuda, 2003).

Emma read, "Ushiro ni iru no dare? [Who is behind me?]"

Emma skipped *kame* when reading *kame-kun* (turtle): "Kun no ushiro ni iru no wa dare. [Who is behind the . . .?]"

"I'm thinking what's that letter!" Emma replied because she was stumped on *kame*.

"Kamekun!" Emma quickly responded.

Here, Emma had difficulty with the word *kame*, which caused her to skip it. When she wanted to go back to fill in the blank, Emma code switched to English to say that she was trying to figure out the graphic information. I also believe that the picture on the page helped in supplying additional information that aided in Emma's final response. The attention to details in written language, or the ways in which she wanted to identify word sounds, spellings, and other graphic cues required serious thought and effort. In these instances, code switching increased when more cognitive work was required on Emma's behalf when reading in Japanese. This observation supports the idea that bilingual children will code switch during cognitively taxing activities (Reyes, 2004). The code switching allowed Emma to rely on a piece of her language ability to supplement another dimension of her developing reading competence.

To provide another powerful example of the linguistic flexibility and cognitive strength of moving between two languages when reading, consider how Emma code switched to retell entire stories. Earlier, I introduced pieces of Emma reading *Kasa* with her father. When she finished reading it to her father, I asked her (in English) to tell me what the story was about. Because I switched to English, Emma did so most likely to accommodate the language preference of the person to whom she was addressing.

"Kasa sashite kaerou [Let's open the umbrella and go home]," Emma read.

"Can you tell me about what you read?" I asked as soon as she finished reading.

"Can you not ask me that?" Emma replied.

"Well it has to be about something. Can you tell me what it was about? I would love to hear about it," I said trying to coax Emma into retelling the story.

"What about . . . what about . . ., " Emma started. "How do you say *kasa* in English? I know. 'Umbrella.' And everyone has different umbrellas. One is red, one is yellow, one is blue, and one is green and one is white that you can see through and one is blue. One is black and one is rainbow and another red one," Emma described.

Emma code switched from the language of the text to the language I used, which is an example of a participant-related code switch. At the same time, within that code switch, and within a matter of seconds, Emma has translated the story through her retelling. There were pieces of the story that did not appear in her retelling. For instance, Emma did not mention that the people in the story had their own colored umbrellas and that they were going home in the rain. However, her retelling does address the major emphasis of the story, which were the different colored umbrellas. Clearly, this example demonstrates how code switching was the result of language flexibility and not language incompetence on the part of one language or the other.

As seen through this perspective, code switching can be viewed as a "thinking tool" that allowed Emma to not only accomplish an immediate, situated activity by finding a solution to a problem that she encountered. Emma was also able to code switch for tactical conversational moves, such as changing the topic, addressing the language of other participants, and emphasizing points that she wanted to make. These short-term goals developed Emma's linguistic repertoire as well as developed her reading ability. While this may be the case, long-term social consequences evolved out of these daily interactions with language, texts, and individuals in her environment.

Switching as Identity Building

The evocation and acceptance of Emma's code switching negotiated, refined, and supported her identity in her early biliteracy. Within a larger social arena, code switching provided her recognition as a reader and as a participant in reading events with Japanese texts embedded within an English and Japanese language context. In other words, the ways in which Emma employed language and how that employment was accepted or rejected within the home linked up to larger possibilities for her to take on multiple roles and to develop relationships through the use of language. While code switching was a verbal act, it was also social action and reaction to other people around her. This point is illustrated through the ways in which code switching evolved and changed over time.

Between 4 to 5 years of age, Emma's code switches were limited. Her Japanese–English code switches were sequential contrasts that sounded like egocentric thought in solving problems. In addition, the majority of her English–Japanese code switches were also sequential contrasts. A small percentage of her code switching involved setting off personal stories that did not relate directly to the text. At this young age, Emma was still an early proficient reader and naturally still trying to make sense of text and what reading involves. Many of Emma's code switches reflected this behavior. She code switched to say things like "I don't need that" as she tried to relate the Japanese phonology and orthography. There were also times, as I presented earlier, when she monitored herself by saying, "No" or "I don't know."

Emma's code-switching patterns, however, changed a year later between the ages of 5 and 6 as they began to diversify. Instead of code switching dominating as a thinking tool, it began to evolve as a conversational tool by which Emma tried to redirect the topic of conversation or project herself differently, such as through joking. Why did code-switching functions evolve over time?

One piece of the explanation lies in the participant boundaries and relationships. In the earlier dialogue, Jay maintained overall control of the conversation. If Emma appeared to be off-task, he tried to pull her back in with phrases such as, "Tsugi wa? [What's next?]." As he did not see her as an independent reader, he read the text to her or directed her through activities. The parent–child relationship was dominated through power relationships in which Jay, the more experienced language user, provided Emma with limited opportunities to direct the conversation.

One year later, the dynamics began to shift. Instead of Jay reading to Emma, he often encouraged Emma to read, which gave Emma more freedom and control in the conversation. Within this freedom, Emma code switched to try to negotiate the topic, or she would reply, "OK, Mister." While power relationships were still embedded, they became more permeable, which allowed Emma to use language for more conversational purposes.

Our relationship with Emma was fluid and shifting as we saw in different ways. When she appeared to be reading, we wanted to pass over the responsibility to her, which gave her more control and power in negotiating topics. Because roles in any social relationship are always shifting, ambiguity exists (Heller, 1988). The presence of ambiguity requires participants to reinterpret and react to new situations; they must perceive events, relate them to what they already know, and act in ways that access them power and acceptance into relationships with other people. As we modified our roles, we co-constructed, with Emma, her roles. This modification of roles became reflected in the evolution of code-switching behaviors.

While we co-constructed Emma's reader identity through Japanese and English texts, she also began to redefine and articulate her social and language identities. Reader, social, and language identities needed to work alongside each other. If Emma did not see herself as a speaker of Japanese, she would not have felt herself to be a reader who was competent and capable enough to read Japanese texts, and the same holds true for English texts. The use of code switching was a way for Emma to work across language boundaries to develop not only those competencies but also to see herself in the roles of reader and language user. In this sense, what is significant about Emma's early bilingual reading is the idea that the local use, acceptance, or rejection of language forms has long-term consequences in how she could perceive her participation and ability as a reader.

Conclusion

Emma used both English and Japanese to navigate texts and participant conversations. In many ways, learning to read for Emma involved language patterns and social roles and relationships that do not always come into our discussions of reading when talking about monolingual readers. While there was an immediate goal to her language use when reading, these goals linked up to larger social consequences that involved reader, social, and language identities.

Here I would like to make a note of caution in fully interpreting Emma's early reading in the context of our home. While our knowledge of how parental interactions around books develops early literacy behaviors, much of which provided a framework for understanding Emma's early reading, we have to be cautious about privileging the storybooks or the typical "bedtime" story as the main pathway into beginning reading. As seen through the snippets of dialogue, Jay and I regularly read with Emma, worked with her, and purchased her books and other reading materials. Heath (1983) was one of the first who warned against assuming that all children are enculturated into these similar literate traditions. Discussing two communities that were only miles apart, Roadville (white working-class community) and Trackton (black working-class community), in the Piedmont Carolinas, Heath described how children in these communities come to school with different types of definitions of, purposes for, and interactions around reading. Heath (1983: 190) wrote about the parents of the Trackton community: "Just as Trackton parents do not buy special toys for their young children, they do not buy books for them either; adults do not create reading and writing tasks for the young, nor do they consciously model or demonstrate reading and writing behaviors for them." Heath painted a different picture of the Roadville parents,

> Roadville wives and mothers buy books for their children and bring home from church Sunday School materials supplied for the young. Before their babies are six months old, Roadville mothers read simple books, usually featuring a single object on each page, to their children ... Within Roadville; the most predictable reading activity in those homes with preschoolers is the bedtime story. (Heath 1983: 222–223)

Heath went on to explain how these enculturations into reading practices translates into the ways in which children interpret reading in school.

Emma's interactions around print sound similar to the Roadville children. Emma always had a parent with whom to read and a variety of picture books to read. Being thousands of miles away from Japan did not stop Emma from receiving storybooks and activity books from her grandmother. While this may be the case, research has shown that this may not be the case for all linguistically diverse families. As can be seen above, Emma was socialized into reading events from a young age and always had a reading partner in Jay or me. Consequently, Emma received similar messages in how one reads, what one reads, and what reading looks and sounds like in both languages and across materials written in English and Japanese. This is not always the case in linguistically diverse families.

Linguistically Diverse Families

Gregory's work with linguistically diverse families in Britain and France suggests that parents carry with them their own interpretations and definitions of learning how to read that has cultural origins, or everyday cultural routines around reading. Children must, in turn, be able to situate themselves within these cultural contexts. Gregory (1996) described how Tony, a young Chinese-speaking boy living in Britain, had to "learn to read" before his father allowed him to have books, an idea that countered Tony's teacher's beliefs about having and reading books. Reading in Chinese for Tony was considered serious work in which memorization of Chinese characters was considered the prerequisite for any type of reading experience by his family. Gregory wrote about the families in her study, "All families view reading as a future investment. Pleasure and satisfaction are seen as the result of hard work and do not belong to the beginning stage of learning to read" (1996: 42).

Some points that summarize some general thoughts about reading within linguistically diverse families are:

- They do perceive reading as important and deem it as a major factor in school success (Bus, 2002; Delgado-Gaitan, 1992).
- Linguistically diverse families who live in English-dominant communities feel that learning to read, write, and speak in English is necessary for school and future economic stability (Gregory, 1996; Martinez-Roldan & Malave, 2004).
- At the same time, they feel that maintaining their heritage language is important to retain membership and connections to their cultural heritage (Gregory, 1996; Gregory et al., 2004).
- They will modify their language to match the language ability of early language learners during reading events (Parke et al., 2002).
- They will attempt to support their children's uses of English in reading and writing (Delgado-Gaitan, 1992; Martinez-Roldan & Malave, 2004).

Thus, children are socialized into reading practices in the home and the community. Reading practices are varied and dynamic among linguistically diverse families and are influenced by culture, community, and beliefs about reading.

Reaction Questions

How do you view Emma's code-switching behaviors? What would you do if you heard Emma code switching during reading events?

Suggested Activities

- Interview a bilingual individual about their code-switching behaviors. Inquire about when and why they code switch. Do they code switch only in conversation or when reading texts? How do they perceive the similarities and differences between the two?
- Observe a group of children with the same native language use their native language and English during a cognitively difficult activity. Is there evidence of code switching? Document the different types of one-word code switches and grammatical code switches. What purposes do the code switches serve (sequential contrast, change in topic, change in the mode of interaction, etc.)? Is it used as a social tool or as a linguistic tool?

Suggested Reading

For additional readings, please refer to the work of the following researchers. On the reading process: Alan Flurkey, Ken Goodman, Yetta Goodman, Frank Smith, and Eric Paulson. On code switching: Peter Auer, Mileidis Gort, John Gumperz, Iliana Reyes, Carol Myers-Scotton, and Lei Wei.

CHAPTER 7

"I Don't Want to Be Japanese Anymore"

When Emma Met School

Emma's entrance into kindergarten saw major evolutions in how she used, viewed, and talked about English and Japanese. In Chapter 6, I alluded to some of these shifts in relation to Emma's identities through the window of her name writing. However, the most prominent moment for me was when Emma said that she did not want to be Japanese three months into kindergarten. As I illustrated throughout previous chapters, Emma was an early proficient reader and writer in Japanese and English who actively engaged in exploring the forms and functions of written language through participating within sets of social relationships with other people. She had what I felt at the time was the means for being successful and adjusting to activities in connection to both languages. And, as the previous chapters suggest, Emma actively negotiated and developed social and linguistic competences.

Yet I had to ask the serious question of why would Emma, an early proficient biliterate child, articulate her desires to lose part of her national and linguistic identities when they only supplemented her growing ability to participate in the world around her? What was happening in school to influence Emma's perceptions of herself as an early biliterate child? In other words, what beliefs did Emma acquire upon entering kindergarten and how did these beliefs surface within Emma's perceptions of herself and reading and writing in English and Japanese?

This chapter will address these questions to better understand what happened when Emma met formal schooling in English. Within this chapter, I will focus on the types of reading and writing to which Emma was introduced in kindergarten and First Grade, how these school-based read-ing and writing practices manifested themselves within Emma's writing in the home, and what they meant toward her becoming biliterate. I will then discuss the ideological tensions that Emma had to negotiate in regard to English and Japanese, which advises a cautionary note about discussing becoming biliterate outside of underlying social and ideological driving forces that are not always immediately visible in our definitions of biliteracy (Martinez-Roldan & Malave, 2004; Schieffelin et al., 1998).

What Is School All About Anyway?

For Emma, like most children, school is about learning how to do things and how to do things according to someone else's rules. Emma attended preschool, which was play-based, for two hours and 45 minutes Monday to Thursday for two years before kindergarten. While preschool provided Emma with certain kindergarten concepts such as circle time, centers, scheduling, and bringing papers back and forth from home and school, she still needed to adjust to the longer days, the intense work time, and other subject/content areas, such as English language arts (ELA) (reading and writing), math, and science.

Emma's school is one of five elementary schools in our district. There were approximately 540 students enrolled in Emma's school at the time of her kindergarten year, and statistics show that out of that number 83% were reported as white, 10% as Hispanic, 6% as Asian, and 1% as African American. Emma's school, as well as the other elementary schools in our district, is considered a high-performing school, meaning that the students in the elementary schools in the school district scored in the top 90th percentile on the New York ELA and math tests (Greatschools, n.d.).

Emma entered kindergarten in September 2003, just one and a half years after the No Child Left Behind (NCLB) Act was signed into law by George W. Bush in January 2002. Needless to say, the effects of NCLB were starting to come into full swing when Emma began kindergarten. In fact, kindergarteners admitted in the 2003 school year were the first group of students who would be tested in every grade from Third Grade (before NCLB, students were tested in Fourth, Sixth, and Eighth Grades in New York) and who would be required to take not only the New York State's math and ELA exams but also the newly developed science and social-studies standardized tests. According to a school newsletter, when Emma was in kindergarten, students lost 17 mornings to tests taking and their teacher for an additional 3–12 days for scoring. On math and ELA test days, the school needed to utilize every teacher in the building, which required the school district to implement a policy where children in Grade

K-2 would have a two-hour delay on one or two days during the week of the math and ELA tests. It is safe to say that Emma entered kindergarten when school started to become about "accountability" on student learning, which was measured by "the test" (Goodman et al., 2004; Kohn, 2000).

As the effects of NCLB influenced the larger schooling context, school was about learning to be a "student" in a time of political accountability (Gee, 1996). This meant that Emma, as well as other new kindergarteners, were required to act like students, to complete work as required by the teacher, and to talk and write like students. When these categories came together, Emma felt a belonging in school, and her kindergarten teacher commented that Emma was a motivated and independent learner.

Adjusting Well to Kindergarten

Emma was the kind of student who, as any teacher would suggest, adjusted well to kindergarten. The phrase "adjusting well to kindergarten" alludes to the notion that Emma emotionally and behaviorally acted like an expected student for her grade and age. On the one hand, Emma willingly participated during small and large groups and completed independent activities without circumstance. Emma exhibited particular behaviors such as raising her hand when she wanted to speak and cooperated with the teacher and the other students. Emma's teacher praised her about how she made friends easily and got along with other students in the class.

On the other hand, the idea of adjusting well to kindergarten also implies that Emma had the capability to follow a routine or a schedule of events within school. Emma's classroom was organized according to daily routines, which included circle time, independent work, ELA, math, centers, specials (i.e. music, library, art, and physical education), lunch, and recess. Emma demonstrated the ability to cope with the curriculum that was embedded within these daily routines. Emma entered into kindergarten when the teachers were not required to use a particular reading basal or reading series, and Emma's teacher integrated a tremendous amount of children's literature. This professional freedom, however, changed by the time Emma's brother Ricky entered kindergarten four years later. When Ricky entered school, the entire kindergarten used a reading series that focused on phonics. The program guided teachers to teach sounds through the use of sound symbols, such as teaching the /ī/ by writing "my" and "high" as mī and hī.

Emma's teacher appeared to have the autonomy to adjust the curriculum in the classroom to fit her *perceived* needs of the children. As a former teacher myself, I acknowledge that I did not get to know the full competencies of each child for the reason that my perceptions of children were always framed by the assessments I used and constrained by the context of the classroom. As a new teacher, I did not have the immediate knowledge or lens to see how children's actions outside the classroom added to their competencies as learners. Similarly, Emma's teacher saw Emma through the work that she provided her. And while the literature set the tone of the classroom, Emma's teacher valued other types of isolated teaching practices such as memorizing sight words, practicing writing words, and testing letter–sound correspondences. In some ways, these regular teaching practices also narrowed what Emma's teacher saw as being "ready" to read before being taught how to read.

In parent–teacher conferences in April, I inquired about the types of instruction Emma was receiving for reading and specifically asked if Emma was participating in guided reading. Although Emma's teacher said that she pulled children to read from leveled books, Emma was not ready for guided reading. Emma's teacher continued to explain that Emma did have good beginning sight vocabulary but would benefit from additional practice, and her immediate concern was to get children "ready" for reading by developing reading skills. Emma's teacher did not want to discourage Emma by placing her in a guided reading situation in which she would not be successful.

But what does reading readiness mean? Chapter 6 countered the illusional idea of reading readiness. By the April parent–teacher conferences, Emma was already reading in the home in both English and Japanese and demonstrated linguistic flexibility through code-switching behaviors. And Emma was successful, but the ideological underpinnings of reading readiness framed how Emma's teacher viewed Emma's ability to read. In fact, Emma's teacher never knew the extent of Emma's Japanese abilities (a point to which I will return) in reading, writing, and speaking for the reason that they did not count in her kindergarten classroom. Instead, what counted was associated with adjusting and accommodating to curricula and scheduled routines and molding into the teacher's perceptions of a reading-ready child. Because Emma was effective on the whole in doing so, it was noted that Emma had "adjusted well to kindergarten."

Today's Homework: Phonic Worksheet

Completing classwork and homework were expected tasks in kindergarten. While classwork was done regularly from the first day of school, Emma's teacher sent homework from January in order to give her kindergarten students time to adjust to in-school routines. Work done in class evolved around projects, center activities, and hands-on engagement in reading activities; participation within these activities did not always result in tangible products. Emma also completed commercialized worksheets for handwriting practice, math, and creating books, and isolated reading skills (such as practicing alphabetic letters) in school. These worksheets were then sent home at the end of the week in Emma's communication folder, which came home on Friday.

Starting from January, homework was also sent home in Emma's communication folder. Particularly in the beginning stages, I helped Emma with her homework, which consisted of handwriting, math, or phonics instruction. In February of her kindergarten year, Emma (5 years, 6 months) brought home a phonics worksheet that focused on writing the beginning letter sound for the provided picture. After I explained the directions to Emma, she started to complete the worksheet on her own. I happened to glance over at her as she was writing the letter "P" in the space in front of the picture that started with the /p/ sound. Emma needed to write the letter "P" using three lines: top-line, baseline, and midline. Without crossing the baseline, Emma wrote the entire P within the mid-line and baseline. I stopped her and suggested that I show her how to use the lines. With a ruler, I drew similar lines and demonstrated how to write "P" using the given lines, and modeled the other letters. Emma then rewrote her "P."

Emma was a prolific writer in the home, as I illustrated in earlier chapters. She understood the purpose of the worksheet but had difficulty utilizing the lines not because she rarely wrote or had little experiences with writing. She ran into trouble because her writing in the home did not match the type and appearance of writing that was expected of her in school. In the home, Emma mostly wrote on white or colored blank paper. There were times when she wrote on lined paper, but she did not strictly associate lined paper with writing and viewed it as a useful medium for drawing. The way in which Emma approached writing in the home was more permeable and open for interpretation. School-based writing was not. In many ways, I saw my role as helping Emma to accustom herself to the nuances of school-based practices that did not always reflect what Emma did in the home.

As Table 7.1 illustrates, I collected 81 pieces of work which were sent home from school in Emma's communication folder. Commercialized worksheets, both done in school and sent home for homework, consisted of 88.1% of the work. Out of the 88.1%, handwriting made up the largest category at 34.5%. After handwriting, worksheets that focused on alphabetic letters and letter–sound relationships was the next largest category at 21.4%, and this category was followed by the focus on individual words. If this amount of work is put into perspective to what Emma was producing in the home, during the same time frame, or between the ages of 5–6 years, Emma produced 63 writing (using both English and Japanese) and drawing artifacts in the home. During the previous year, between the ages of 4–5, Emma created 82 writing and drawing artifacts in the home. Emma

Table 7.1 The amount and types of work sent home in Emma's communication folder in kindergarten.

| | Types | | |
Content	Commercial	Self-written	Total
Handwriting practice	34.5%	0%	29
Writing numbers	3.6%	0%	3
Writing the alphabet	21.4%	0%	18
Making commercially produced books	8.3%	11.9%	17
Writing words	11.9%	0%	10
Writing sentences	8.4%	0%	4
Total	**88.1%**	**11.9%**	**81**

completed more worksheets during her kindergarten year (at least those that were sent home) than writing and drawing artifacts in the home, which dropped from the previous year.

In addition to the commercialized worksheets, Emma also brought home teacher-made journals (11.9% of the total work). Emma's journals were places for exploration and free writing and drawing. In Emma's initial journal, she wrote by writing strings of lines. As her entries progressed, she moved to writing strings of letters and eventually to writing more developed sentences. Her entries were consistently filled with colored pictures that related to her written thoughts. It is interesting to see the progression of Emma's writing over her kindergarten year. In spite of the fact that Emma was already writing in Japanese and English, her initial entries consisted of lines that represented written language. These lines gave way to strings of letters. It was not until December that Emma's written entries were close to readable. These observations led me to believe that Emma needed to become used to the function of journaling before she felt comfortable exploring how written languages work within the media of the journals.

Journals were for writing for oneself, not necessarily for others. In the home, Emma engaged in real-life writing activities for others; she wrote a variety of cards and personal letters, and she drew pictures for other people. This shift in focus was an obstacle for Emma that she quickly overcame, but she needed the time to explore the ideas of why she was writing in a journal: who was the audience, what would that person be interested in, or what was she to write about? If all texts are dialogic, addressing the writer and the audience, then Emma was missing a piece of the puzzle that required some work to solve. By December, Emma overcame those obstacles, which resulted in her actions aligning to the teacher's thoughts about needing the time in the first part of kindergarten to become accustomed to the routines of schools.

"Talk-the-Talk": Negotiation between Japanese and English

Speaking, reading, and writing in English were the preferred media of communication within Emma's school. English allowed students to talk the talk of school. On Emma's home-language survey, which is sent home to every new incoming student to inquire about the home language, I reported that both English and Japanese were used in the home. As I discussed earlier, by kindergarten, Emma felt more comfortable using English over Japanese. This dominance was immediately evident, which placed Emma out of any consideration for English as a second-language service. At the same time, Emma's kindergarten teacher did not know the extent of Emma's Japanese abilities. At the April conferences, Emma's teacher mentioned that Emma talked about Japanese school.

Emma did not have the opportunity to speak Japanese in kindergarten because there was no one else in the class to whom she could speak. She did, however, attempt to write in some Japanese by writing her name in *hiragana*. During her kindergarten year, she wrote her name in both English and *hiragana* on 35% of her schoolwork that came home and on her homework. The first time I observed Emma's writing her name in both scripts occurred one night when she completed the phonics worksheet that I described earlier. After Emma completed the worksheet, she wrote her name in *hiragana* and then in Roman alphabet. When I questioned her actions, she replied, "Because I'm the only one in my class who can speak Japanese so nobody will know what I'm writing but me." Emma's comment revealed her shifted perceptions of Japanese from that November night when she questioned her identity.

Emma recognized that Japanese was a tool for inclusion and exclusion, and that she could employ it as a means of acquiring access into groups or of denying access into parts of her social network which was defined by the use of Japanese. The ways in which Emma presented herself were partial; her actions were fragmented because of the sense of herself that she had built over time was in conflict (Moje & Luke, 2009). She was resistant to her Japanese while there were other times when she viewed it as an asset. These conflicting notions required negotiation, which resulted in Emma's freedom and ability to select how and when she wanted to portray particular outward appearances in regard to language, which was always influenced by the constraints of contextual influences. The context of school pushed Emma to consider these negotiations in a new way.

Emma's teacher acknowledged Emma's ability to write her name in both languages, which she observed her doing in class. During the April parent–teacher conferences, Emma's teacher described it as "refreshing," without any further elaboration. Over time, I have contemplated the term "refreshing" and what it was meant to signify. I have come to the conclusion that Emma's teacher enjoyed watching Emma exhibit some of these biliterate behaviors to the end that they did not interfere with Emma's English abilities. In other words, Emma's teacher most likely felt that Emma did not fall into the category of an English language learner who needed English support in the classroom. Emma could handle the English medium of the curriculum and still display her Japanese abilities. A lack of communication between teacher and student did not exist, which allowed Emma to talk like a student and to write like a student in the privileged language of communication: English.

Welcome to First Grade

While kindergarten was framed by the idea of adjustment to school, First Grade was characterized by the notion that students should be reading by the end of the year. This tone was set before Emma left kindergarten. At Emma's kindergarten parent–teacher conferences in April, Emma's teacher stated that while students were not pushed to read by the end of kindergarten, they were expected to be reading by the end of their first-grade year. Emma's first-grade teacher emphasized literature, reading, and writing in the classroom and took an integrated approach to the curriculum. When I asked Emma about her reflections of elementary school after entering middle school, she quickly commented that her first-grade teacher was her favorite (next to her fifth-grade teacher). The highlight of the year, which Emma has taken with her throughout her years of schooling, was the restaurant, The Funky Monkey Café, which Emma's teacher organized and to which all the parents were invited. The class read about animals and their habitats, went to the grocery store to buy food, and created menus, placemats, decorations, and other materials that they needed to convert their classroom into a restaurant. This type of integrated and holistic approach to the curriculum created an authentic engagement with reading, writing, and learning that heightened Emma's positive experiences in the classroom her first-grade year.

While this may be the case, other trends that started in kindergarten continued. With the focus on having children read by the end of First Grade, emphasis was placed on skills that were deemed necessary for reading. These skills were taught through worksheets which were done at school and as homework. In addition to the persistent use of commercialized worksheets, the uses of English and Japanese not only in school but also in the home continued to evolve. Underlying these shifts were ideological tensions around language and its tie to identity and access to school and, in particular, to First Grade, which Emma felt was her most memorable year.

Teaching Reading and Writing

Similar to kindergarten, Emma completed classwork in the form of work-sheets. The majority of first-grade worksheets, however, came out of workbooks created by publishing companies. The teacher tore out the pages that needed to be completed, and the students did so as part of the classroom routine. These workbook pages, as well as photocopied work-sheets, were also sent home for homework. Unlike kindergarten, Emma received homework by the end of September and completed it anywhere from two to three times a week. Home reading also became an integral part of homework. Emma could read either by herself or with me, and I had to sign the home reading log to acknowledge that Emma read.

Emma's first-grade year saw a drastic increase in the amount of com-pleted work (both schoolwork and homework) sent home in her com-munication folder. As Table 7.2 illustrates, I collected 562 pieces of work that were sent home over the course of First Grade, and 94% of those 562 were worksheets or workbook pages. I combined any type of math-related work under the general category of math, which comprised 40% of Emma's completed work sent home. The other 60% focused on ELA, more specifically on reading, writing, speaking, and listening. Table 7.2 further

Table 7.2 The amount and types of work sent home in Emma's communication folder in First Grade.

Content	Types		
	Commercial	Self-written	Total
Math worksheets	40.0%	0%	225
English Language Arts	53.5%	6%	337
Total	93.5%	6%	562
Further breakdown of the English Language Arts Work			
Fill in blanks	8.9%	0%	50
Writing and matching words	26.9%	0%	151
Worksheets that address following directions	3.6%	0%	20
Sheets that addressed the classroom science or social-studies theme	6.4%	0%	35
Reading comprehension	5.9%	0%	33
Writing alphabet letters	1.8%	0%	10
Self-writing such as journals or sentences with spelling words	0%	6.0%	38
Totals	**53.5%**	**6.0%**	**337**

breaks down ELA into smaller categories in order to gain a better sense of the focus of the work Emma was asked to do.

The largest category of worksheets centered on individual words. These workbook pages were typical in the sense that Emma had to circle the word with a certain beginning letter sound or vowel sound. Word families were another big piece of the word-oriented view of worksheets. Emma had to fill in sentences with words from the word families for that week or had to complete worksheets that asked her to match word families.

After the focus on words, 5.9% of completed worksheets addressed reading comprehension. These worksheets tended to be commercialized and photocopied. Emma needed to read, or I read to her, a short four-sentence paragraph after which she had to answer five questions related to the passage. The other type of reading concentrated on following directions (3.6%) that required Emma to read sentences and to follow the directions of the sentence. Some 6.4% of completed worksheets were related to curricular themes, such as animals or seasons. Unlike the other categories that appeared to serve the sole purpose of progressing reading skills, these worksheets involved reading and writing that served the specific purpose of developing thematic units.

In addition to worksheets, Emma brought home some pieces that consisted of self-writing (6%). One such example is represented in Figure 7.1. In Figure 7.1, which Emma completed in school, she wrote sentences and underlined the sight words that needed to be included in the sentence. Within this regular classroom activity, Emma had to write two sentences using predetermined words. While some sentences were meaningful, such as those in Figure 7.1, others, while they served the purpose of the activity, were not authentic sentences. For instance, in Figure 7.2, Emma wrote, "The cat is fat" because she included words from the -at word family. In

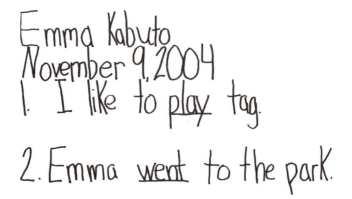

Figure 7.1 Emma (6 years, 3 months) wrote sentences in school underlining the sight word.

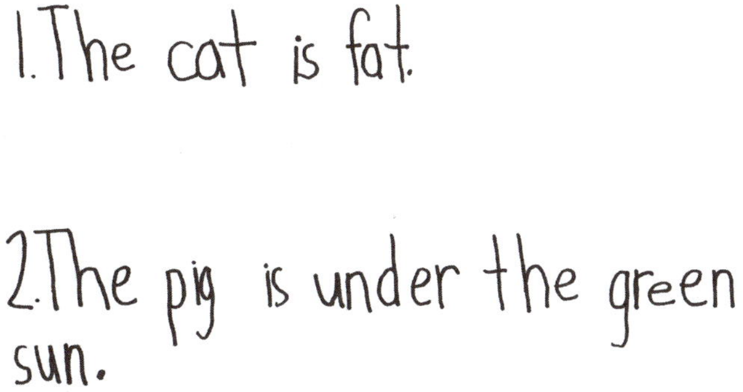

1. The cat is fat.

2. The pig is under the green sun.

Figure 7.2 Emma (6 years, 5 months) wrote sentences that included -*at* and -*ig* words and the sight word "green."

the second sentence, Emma wrote, "The pig is under the green sun," in order to include a word from -*ig* family and the color sight word green. These sentences, in fact, were similar to the commercialized worksheets with a word focus, which constrained the vocabulary and the voice of the writer. By writing these types of sentence, Emma created controlled, monosyllabic text that had little to do with who she was as a cultural, social, and emotional individual participating in the multiple communities that organized in her life.

Shifts to School-Based Writing Practices

From First Grade, the types of reading and writing that Emma did in school were the antithesis of what she did in the home. Emma's writing in the home was original; it was about Emma as a young developing biliterate child. This social core of Emma's writing created a mutual relationship with the forms that her writing took. Consequently, between the ages of 4 and 6, writing in Japanese and English was a common feature of Emma's beginning writing. Even in kindergarten, when Emma was trying to work out the tensions in how she could present herself through languages, Emma's action suggested that she saw the benefits of speaking, reading, and writing in Japanese. In Emma's kindergarten year, I collected a total of 63 writing and drawing samples in the home. Out of these 63 samples, 58.7% were written in English, 31.7% were written in Japanese, and 4.8% were in both languages (see Table 2.1).

These behaviors changed drastically when Emma was in First Grade. When Emma was in First Grade, I collected 93 writing and drawing samples in the home compared to the 556 worksheets that I collected from school. This number is the second largest number over the four years of data collection, which was proceeded by 134 samples which were collected when Emma was between the ages of 3 and 4. At the same time, out of the 93 samples that I collected, 88.2% were written in English while 3.2% were written in Japanese. Not only was there a drastic decrease in Emma's uses of written Japanese, Emma's writing began to reflect school-based practices, which never appeared in her writing in the home when she was in kindergarten.

Earlier, I introduced Emma's sentences in Figure 7.2, which included the words "cat," "fat," "pig," and "green." Emma took this content and created writing pieces that looked liked writing she did in school in Figure 7.3. In Figure 7.3, Emma (6 years, 5 months) wrote words with the short /a/ sound, which included words from -at, -an, -as, and -am word families. Under her list of words, she created math sentences. On the left-hand side, Emma wrote sentences whose sum equals 10, and on the right-hand side, she wrote subtraction sentences whose difference equals 10. The two largest categories of work, the focus on math and individual words, are both represented on this one paper.

There were times when Emma played school during which she was the teacher who created worksheets for imaginary students. This sample was not the result of one of those occasions. Instead, she created this sample in her free time, and she wrote many more like them. By writing school-based

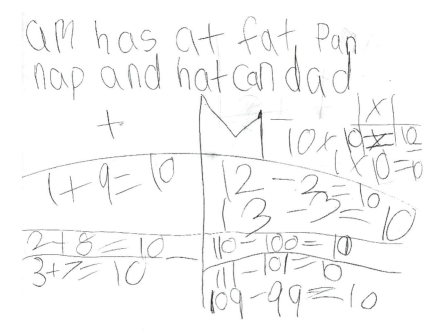

Figure 7.3 Emma (6 years, 5 months) replicated school-based work in the home.

practices, Emma was recreating an autonomous model of literacy reflected in the worksheets she completed in school (Street & Street, 1991). An autonomous model of literacy focuses on a skill-based view of reading and writing isolated from individuals as social and cultural beings. As I have illustrated, texts mediated Emma's identities, and these particular instances when Emma wrote like a student in the home were not any different. By writing autonomous literacy skills, Emma was acquiring membership into school and what school was all about.

Worksheets and isolated practices around word families that have nothing to do with Emma's real family mediated the ways in which Emma constructed and evolved particular identities. The result of this active, social process was Emma's movement away from Japanese in the home and the movement toward school-based writing practices, which sustained a level of membership and acceptance into school.

By the end of First Grade, Emma was reading and was, as her teacher described, a confident writer. Emma's first-grade teacher commented on her ability to write five or more sentences using sight vocabulary and phonetic spellings. In terms of reading, Emma's teacher noted that she developed a substantial sight vocabulary and monitored her reading. However, Emma needed to work on decoding skills, especially for short vowels. Emma's teacher praised Emma for her independence as a reader and writer and said that she had a positive attitude toward school.

Ideological Struggles in Becoming Biliterate

What school privileged and the texts that Emma produced as a result had nothing to do with the knowledge and identities that Emma actively constructed at home before entering kindergarten and First Grade. School was primarily about acquiring membership into a community that had particular ways of doing, talking, acting, and thinking. In actuality, Emma's biliteracy was irrelevant to school; becoming biliterate was counterproductive to becoming a student.

Bilingual Writing and Ideological Tensions

The shifts in Emma's uses of English and Japanese suggest the ideological tensions that she needed to work through at the crossroads of home and school. Ideological contestation refers to the ways Emma acquired, worked through, and reproduced unexamined beliefs and assumptions around languages. Emma's schooling experiences were not immune to the national movement toward English-only learning in schools in the USA, which contends that the only acceptable way to educate linguistically diverse children is through the medium of English (Auerbach, 1993). The underlying power within the English-only ideology privileges English over other languages within school settings.

While Emma recognized the importance of English and Japanese in connecting with family and community, which was the result of being an active member in the home around literacy, she came in contact with something different in school. School was not about building relationships with the words that were embedded within her family; it was about building relationships with word families, specifically those in English (Taylor, 2009). As Emma ventured out of the home and into school, her initial language beliefs came in contact with those connected to educational institutions. In the process of language contact, Emma's early language belief systems began to compete with those of the school. These ideological contestations surfaced in Emma's name writing in kindergarten. Although Emma said that she did not want to be Japanese in November, by February, Emma was writing her name in English and Japanese on her schoolwork and homework. Emma was testing particular ways of presenting herself through writing in the home and school contexts. For this reason, bilingual writing was a trend in her kindergarten year.

By putting herself out there through writing, Emma began to measure the social significance on the ways in which language enacted particular identities and how these enactments allowed her access into different social structures or context-specific domains (Spitulnik, 1998). The result of Emma's active recreation of her identities through bilingual writing was the initiation of a process by which she evaluated the importance of her developing biliteracy in school. Many of Emma's kindergarten teacher's comments suggest that while she recognized Emma's biliterate behaviors, they did not count toward the curriculum in school. Emma's teacher was more concerned with reading readiness, sight words, and social behaviors than other hidden biliterate abilities that contributed to Emma's overall reading and writing growth. The connections between reading, writing, identity, nationality, and family never surfaced within the schoolwork that Emma was asked to do. The consequence was that Emma placed little value on her biliteracy.

First Grade, however, saw the appearance of another trend: language valuation. Language valuation was the process by which Emma placed social value on English over her biliteracy and began to reproduce particular unexamined beliefs around English (Spitulnik, 1998). The result of this process was the shift from biliterate behaviors to English and the appearance of "one-nation, one-language" ideologies in spite of the fact that Emma attended Japanese school on Saturdays during her kindergarten and first-grade years (Tollefson, 1991). Even in Japanese school, Emma wrote her name in *katakana* as a way to place herself outside of the Japanese school structure in the attempt to recognize that she is American as well as Japanese. At the same time, Emma began to comment that because she lives in America, she needed to speak English.

At the same time, school rewarded Emma for her shifting belief systems around language and her abilities to align her reading and writing behaviors toward school-based practices. Emma's first-grade teacher acknowledged that Emma possessed a positive attitude toward school and progressed toward being a confident reader and writer. These competencies were based on autonomous skills related to reading and writing and not necessarily the ways in which reading and writing defined her as a unique, independent child becoming biliterate. In fact, Emma kept her early biliterate capacities hidden from her first-grade teacher, with the reasoning that her school is in New York, which is in America, and requires the capability to speak, read, and write in English.

Home and School as Private and Public Domains

When Emma entered school in kindergarten, she participated within a sociocultural space that was representative of a larger dominant institutional practice. Emma's participation in school was more than learning curricula; it was about being a certain type of person (Gee, 1996). Although I argued that within school bilingual writing was not always valued, I do not believe that Emma lost the importance of Japanese. Instead, the more experienced Emma became with using language in a variety of social domains, the more she learned about the benefits and limitations of Japanese and English to gain acceptance into social structures and with other people.

Instead, Emma's biliteracy became refined, or audience- and context-specific, as it slowly fell into public and private spheres (Rodriguez, 2004). English was the way to communicate in school and within American society; it provided her with power into making her voice heard. Emma's biliteracy, on the other hand, was a private means for connecting to family and friends. Emma's writing samples in Chapter 5 illustrated how writing in two languages allowed her to stretch to many audiences. Emma wrote her family flower (Figure 5.10) when she was 7 years, 11 months old and her card to me (Figure 5.6) when she was 7 years, 5 months old, in Japanese and English to address the voices of those to whom she was writing. For the people who valued her biliteracy and to those who Emma knew could not communicate in English, Emma's biliterate behaviors provided her with an advantage or, as Chapters 6 and 7 described, with social competencies. Entrance in school forced Emma to slowly create a distinction between public and private domains. The public domain was about reproducing dominant ideologies about English as a power-driven discourse, while the private domain was a place for agency, a place to challenge the social structures and the constraints that English placed on her sense of self in relation to family and friends.

Conclusion

Emma's participation in school highlighted the ideological struggles that she encountered as an early biliterate child gaining acceptance into school. Becoming biliterate was not detached from the larger social, cultural, and ideological educational policies that support oral proficiency, reading, and writing in English (Auerbach, 1993; Halcon, 2001; Schieffelin et al., 1998; Woolard, 1998). Many of these ideologies around language and literacy were transmitted through day-to-day interactions with schoolwork and homework. The sheer enormity and quantity of work that focused on the transmission of isolated skills affected the ways in which Emma used languages. In the act of doing, Emma developed identities that aligned herself with group membership into school; she learned how to write, act, talk, and read like a student.

While Emma's involvement in school encouraged writing in English through school-based literacy practices that had little to do with Emma's cultural and language identities, the circumstances that framed Emma's biliteracy were more complicated. There was evidence in her first-grade year that suggests Emma acknowledged that her biliteracy had symbolic value. Becoming biliterate embarked on a private domain, as compared to the public persona that English portrayed.

In many ways, Emma's experiences in becoming biliterate coincide with other case studies that describe biliteracy as an ideological struggle between beliefs and concepts of language use (Halcon, 2001; Martinez-Roldan & Malave, 2004). Martinez-Roldan & Malave (2004) suggest that young biliterate children may acquire English at the expense of children's native language because they develop beliefs and attitudes that contradict the goal of biliteracy. Parents may influence this process by encouraging their children to speak English in the home rather than their native language and by promoting English as the means for social mobility. However, when comparing Emma's experiences with other studies, Jay's and my goal for Emma was to become biliterate. And yet, contestation between the notions and benefits of monolingualism and bilingualism was still a characteristic that defined how and why Emma used English and Japanese. Learning language was more than a transmission of skills and knowledge; it was, most importantly, understanding the larger perspective of how languages organize one's life into meaningful experiences.

Reaction Question

As a classroom teacher, how would you react to Emma writing her name in English and Japanese?

Suggested Activities

1. Interview a young bilingual child about how they use languages in home and school. List the ways in which the child distinguishes languages within private and public domains. What are the properties of those domains? How do those properties influence the ways in which the child uses written and spoken language?

2. Brainstorm ways in which you could supplement worksheets with culturally responsive materials. In your brainstorming, address the following questions:
   - Why would teachers use worksheets for classwork and homework?
   - What are other activities that you could use to supplement worksheets?
   - How would you communicate those activities to parents?

CHAPTER 8

The Journey of Becoming Biliterate

In the beginning of the semester, I ask the classroom teachers, some of whom teach in linguistically diverse classrooms, who enter my graduate classes the following questions:

- What does it mean to be biliterate?
- How do you think children become biliterate?
- Do you think that children should be taught in their first language or be allowed to use multiple languages in the schools? Why or why not?

Some of the themes that came out of their responses are:

- **On being biliterate:** Many teachers feel a person who is biliterate must be able to read and write in two languages. Some teachers acknowledge that while some individuals may be able to speak in a language other than English, they may not be able to read or write in the language. Conversely, while individuals may be able to read in a language other than English, they may not be able to speak that language. Overall, the majority of responses indicate that there must be some degree of fluency in communicating through writing and understanding through reading in order to obtain the title of biliterate.
- **On becoming biliterate:** Teachers are less sure of how children become biliterate. Many teachers contend that in order to become biliterate children must come from or be born in another country. By pure association with another nationality, children have the potential

to become biliterate. Other teachers feel that children partake in an active process in childhood but are unsure of how to describe that process. This reaction causes teachers to suggest that biliteracy is the result of being raised or immersed in societies that either foster biliteracy or provide a language different from the child's first language because they can maintain their first language while developing a second language.

- **On being taught in two or more languages:** The responses to this question are wide in range. Some teachers feel that if children are taught in their first language, it will disrupt their learning in their second language. Other teachers argue that being taught in multiple languages is a necessity as our country becomes more diverse. Bilingual education, they feel, is beneficial as it allows students to learn other forms of communication and to keep their identities and cultures. Other teachers respond that the question of bilingual education is irrelevant to them, or they do not know what they think about bilingual education.

The impressions that Emma left behind in becoming biliterate have shown that the experiences of early biliterate children are relevant to all of us as classroom teachers, scholars, and educators. Children such as Emma do not leave their histories at the door when they enter our classrooms; they are not blank slates waiting to be drawn upon. Only skimming the surface of biliteracy, the responses to the questions above undermine the depth and irrevocably complex nature of what it means to become biliterate. Traveling though history to revisit Emma's experiences from 3 to 7 years of age, the lasting impression of Emma becoming biliterate have shown me no less.

The House that Emma Built

Becoming biliterate took work, both interpersonal and intrapersonal. It involved physical and cultural tools that gave Emma the opportunity to bridge the parts of her existence: her history, the present, and her future. To provide a brief metaphor, think about building a house. In order to build a house, we need to prepare ourselves with certain things. We will need physical tools: hammers, saws, wood, nails, to name a few. But we will also need plans. Our plans are based on interest and our tastes; we may prefer a ranch or colonial style house, or we may want sliding doors or french doors. While we work in the present, our past experiences may influence the type of house we will build, and we work knowing that our endeavors today will provide us with shelter and safety in the future. Most importantly, we need a space, a place to explore and to put that house together.

While I have oversimplified a very complex project in construction, in connecting this metaphor to becoming biliterate, the tools are written language; that is, the tools that children employ in their quest for meaning and existence. The house is their identity: their sense of self that they create through the use of those tools. Within this book, I have attempted to present Emma's house and how the interworkings of a system of tools recreated identities. And yet, when Emma entered school, the schooling curricula could not get past the tools, or provide a space for building, exploring, and evolving Emma's house. Instead, Emma's house needed to look like everybody else's; there was little room for a house that deviated from the curriculum. My findings raised serious concerns about how the ways in which children are taught perpetuates inequalities in how they are educated; in fact, some children may not have the opportunity to build their houses because they are continually encouraged to sharpen their tools without ever employing them.

Language and Identity

The word "language" is probably one of the most ambiguous terms. Language has taken the overarching connotation of verbal communication, in which we, as humans, have a specialized system of codes or symbols used for a means of representation (Wilson, 1998). Naturally, there are more culture-specific languages, such as English, Japanese, Spanish, Hebrew, etc., that have their own internal structures, codes, and symbols. Chapter 1 introduced the idea that language in this manner of speaking should be viewed as a system of cultural tools. What is needed is a better understanding of how language as a cultural tool represents Language (with the big L) as a mechanism for authenticating the existence of children's lives and creating a cohesive purpose for them to grow and develop as individuals.

The notion of biliteracy, which is built on theories of language and literacy, follows the same suit. And the teachers' responses to the questions that opened this chapter suggest that their understandings of biliteracy are tied to being able to read and write fluently: the tools. Current research highlights how the partnerships between literacy, identity, and culture forge a compelling case for acknowledging how language as a cultural tool system enact identities in socially specific contexts (Moje & Luke, 2009). Emma's experiences have illustrated this point throughout this book: Emma used English and Japanese written forms to create narratives about her life, and these narratives became part of Emma's history as a writer (Sfard & Prusak, 2005).

Emma's writing told a persuasive story about how her life was deeply woven with her history, which was a force in defining her personal development and acculturation in the home, community, and school in the present. There were several stories within that narrative that required an arrangement of sorts, and it was through a synchronization of the many words and ways of doing things that Emma could arrange her life into meaningful spaces (Holquist, 1981). Becoming biliterate, in turn, involved synchronization of the many practices in which Emma became involved. Early biliterate children, like Emma, have the potential to become strikingly socially savvy in accounting for the differences in what social contexts have to offer and how the ways in which the world informs their biliterate behaviors. In fact, Emma created a repertoire of literate behaviors that she could exhibit depending on her interest, who she was interacting with, and the context in which she was engaged.

Journey of Self-Discovery

Becoming biliterate for Emma was a journey. From birth, Emma saw and interacted with people and things around her through written language. Because Emma was born into a biliterate home, she encountered things around her in English and Japanese and used language to build relationships, enter into relationships, and make sense of the ways in which languages organized her life.

Life for Emma was made up of an endless amount of possibilities. Writing provided a means to document the everyday happenings of the world around her. In some ways, writing in English and Japanese allowed Emma to jot down to herself how different concepts emerged; she could explore new connections and expand the scope of her thoughts. This idea was clearly evident in the new ways in which she viewed the potentialities of scripts. The realization that *hiragana* could be used to write her Japanese friends' and her family's names evolved Emma's writing into certain states of actualization of what life meant to herself and to other people. Over time, Emma's employment of Japanese and English defined her self-in-practice—the active recreation of identity though the designing of texts. When Emma wrote in two languages, she reinforced her identity as a biliterate child. Conversely, participation in school required Emma to redefine how English connected to her current experiences. While she spoke, read, and wrote in English from the time she was 2 years old, the substance of English she encountered in school was different to what she had previously experienced. In many ways, it did not match the combination of English and Japanese in which she was experienced. In other words, Emma saw an otherness in her identity.

This sense of otherness manifested itself in the ways in which Emma talked about how English and Japanese allowed her access into not only school but also American society (Kristeva, 2003). Gee (2004) described the ways in which we, as individuals, can "despise" ourselves, which will lead to "dynamics where there is more than one person in us." He stated, "We are multiple people. We have different identities, and those identities don't have to be compatible with each other. They can be at war with each other" (2004). As Emma ventured out into the world, she did not always feel that she belonged to particular social groups or structures. When she said that she did not want to be Japanese anymore, it was not because she did not have access into English-speaking social structures or felt that Japanese was irrelevant in her life. In fact, two months later, Emma began writing her name in Japanese next to the English representation of her name.

These observations, along with many more, led me to argue that writing is a tool to develop spaces of possibility in an ever-changing world. Emma could be the unique person she was (and is) and could accommodate the ways in which life forced her to be "multiple people," which allowed her to endure life's changes and to enter freely into public and private spaces; writing in two languages liberated Emma from the constraints of ideological beliefs that monolingualism was tied to social competence. Instead, she has shown how writing in two languages creates a social competence above and beyond monolingual abilities.

Thus, as Emma worked through a variety of circumstances that her changing environment created, she had to work through linguistic, social, and cultural changes. With change came possibility: the possibility to bring what she already experienced to new spaces by meshing public and private domains or multiple participatory spaces (Dyson, 1993; Gee, 2005). Emma did this over and over in her writing. As she entered new spaces, such as school, or when new spaces were brought to her, such as the birth of her brother, they worked their way into and through her writing. She used writing to consider her interpretation of the world and who she was in it, and English and Japanese acted as transformative agents in understanding and enduring change by working through and challenging the tensions that arose from participating in these complementary and contradictory spaces (Taylor, 2005). As Hoffman articulated, "When I write, I have a real existence that is proper to the activity of writing—an existence that takes place midway between me and the sphere of artifice, art, pure language. This language is beginning to invent another me" (1989: 121).

Interworkings of the Social and the Mental

Hoffman alludes to the idea that language was a way to create an existence that does not always have to conform to social norms and dominant views. In many ways, there is a complex interplay between the written language, identities, and beliefs systems. Emma's school-based writing clearly demonstrated the ways in which writing constrained how she could portray herself. She was limited to sight words, controlled vocabulary, and literal level comprehension sheets.

These types of practices were context-specific ways of using language. Emma learned how to be a particular type of "student" who had a role in the classroom structure by writing like that type of student. The localized participation in school-based discourses allowed her to fit the mold of an ideal student but also countered the notion of becoming biliterate. This process supports the argument that becoming a member of a particular community of practice requires negotiation and participation in language-based processes (Barton & Tusting, 2005). If this is the case, without theories of language, little is added to the discursive process of how one becomes a member of communities.

Emma's code switching showed how the integration of code-switching frameworks illuminated the ways in which Emma actively engaged in reading events. She gained membership as a reader. A code-switching lens re-established the argument that the movement between languages was the result of language competence to problem solve difficult areas and social competence as Emma maneuvered conversational and social roles with reading acts. More importantly, these localized actions negotiated Emma's reader identities. Grasping the full extent of how text recreates identities necessitates the integration of theories of language outside of sociocultural theory.

Biliteracy (with the Big "B")

Instead of making the written language tools synonymous with the definition of biliteracy, more room is needed in order to foreground freedom in selecting, choosing, and legitimizing identities, families, and beliefs around languages. The latter is distinctive from the former and is what defines Biliteracy (with the big "B"). It is biliteracy as a tool system that allows children to become Biliterate; it allows children to think and act in the world. If becoming Biliterate is positioned as a right that children have, then three points should frame this view:

1. Children need the opportunity to develop a full-embodied identity.
2. Children can freely choose their mode of learning and expression.
3. Children are encouraged to become aware of their own thinking.

Children Need the Opportunity to Develop a Full-Embodied Identity

Emma's experiences reveal that exploration, development, and socialization into early biliteracy encouraged a fully embodied identity in which she was able to work through linguistic and social tensions, define who she was, and understand others in relation to herself through the physical, or embodied, use of writing. Freire writes, "Education as the practice of freedom—as opposed to education as the practice of domination—denies that man is abstract, isolated, independent, and unattached to the world; it also denies that the world exists as a reality apart from people" (2003: 81). Teaching as the practice of freedom recognizes that children come to school with tools from homes and families and that these tools can be transformative agents in children understanding what they see as they enter new spaces and endure life's changes over time and spaces.

With mandated educational policies there are limits to the room that children have to work through the changes that they perceive. They are constrained by scripted texts that draw them back to the task at hand, without giving the flexibility to take on new roles and voices. Current curricula address ways in which teachers can respond to the invention of reading problems. There is no response to the social inequalities that children face, the economic disparities of schools that are labeled "at risk," and the Language identities and family histories that children bring with them to the classroom. Mandated polices justify "inert ideas" (Whitehead, 1929) or recreate the "banking system" (Freire, 2003) of education. The possibilities of creating those houses are no longer endless.

Children Can Freely Choose Their Mode of Learning and Expression

Emma was successful because she was able to freely choose her mode of learning and expression from a range of possibilities. By observing her write and by the number of writing artifacts that I collected over the years, I have concluded that Emma was drawn to written language. This was a preferred mode for her to learn about herself and the world around her. However, I do not want to privilege written language as the only mode of learning (Kress, 1997; Leland & Harste, 1994); over the years, as I have watched my son grow as a language user, I have come to truly appreciate the semiotic nature of learning. Unlike Emma, he was drawn to blocks, Legos, and other types of physical objects that took on sociocultural meanings such as bowling, roller coasters, and balloons. At 3 years, 5 months of age, my son did not know how to write his name in either language, while Emma wrote her name in English at 3 years, 2 months and Japanese at 4 years, 5 months. As a society we tend to privilege the written forms of language over others that are meaningful to children. We look for the first letter-like forms or the stringing together of letters into words. Mandated programs try to "teach this" by making children fit into a particular mode of what all students should be like. However, they ignore the fact that children find different things important. As Whitehead explains, "Importance depends on endurance. Endurance is the retention through time of an achievement of value" (1925: 194). Mandated programs ignore the value that freely choosing modes of expression has on "importance," which has been determined by political agendas unrelated to the lives of the children we teach.

Children Are Encouraged to Become Aware of Their Own Thinking

Recognizing and legitimatizing Emma's freedom of thought, expression, and consciousness allowed her to move forward, provided her access to, and encouraged her to learn how to use English and Japanese in a variety of contexts. Between the very young ages of 3 to 7 years, Emma became a critical thinker who engaged in real-life challenges and struggles around learning in two languages; she raised questions, wrote relationships, and challenged dominant ways of using language. Through writing she was able to develop agency by engaging in personal and social conversations that furthered her understandings of written language both socially and linguistically.

Positioning Biliteracy as a right forces us to critically rethink the role of literacy in school. It also demands a revisitation of pedagogy and curricula that involves partnerships between families and communities and that allows children to build their houses. Biliteracy is a person's life history and future; it is a form of expression, and by justifying that we can acknowledge the lives, the families, and the homes of all children. By educational institutions and governmental policies acknowledging the social fabric and dynamics of Biliteracy, we can build bridges between linguistically diverse families and schools to teach for social justice and the rights of children everywhere.

References

Adams, M. J. (1994). Modeling the connections between word recognition and reading. In R. B. Ruddell, M. R. Ruddell, & H. Singer (Eds.), *Theoretical models and processes of reading* (4th ed.) (pp. 838–863). Newark, Del.: International Reading Association.

Auer, P. (1999a). Introduction: Bilingual conversation revisited. In P. Auer (Ed.), *Code-switching in conversation* (pp. 1–24). London and New York: Routledge.

—— (Ed.). (1999b). *Code-switching in conversation*. London and New York: Routledge.

Auerbach, E. R. (1993). Reexamining English only in ESL classrooms. *TESOL Quarterly, 27*, 9–32.

Baghban, M. (1984). *Our daughter learns to read and write: A case study from birth to three.* Newark, Del.: International Reading Association.

—— (2007). Scribbles, labels, and stories: The role of drawing in the development of writing. *Young Children*, November, pp. 20–26.

Barton, D., & Tusting, K. (Eds.). (2005). *Beyond communities of practice: Language, power, and social context.* Cambridge: Cambridge University Press.

Bialystok, E., & Hakuta, K. (1994). *In other words: The science and psychology of second-language acquisition.* New York: Basic Books.

Bourdieu, P. (1991). *Language and symbolic power.* Cambridge, Mass.: Harvard University Press.

Bus, A. (2002). Joint caregiver–child storybook reading: A route to literacy development. In S. Neuman & D. Dickinson (Eds.), *Handbook of early literacy research* (pp. 179–191). New York: Guilford Press.

Campbell, R. (1982). *Dear zoo.* New York: Little Simon.

Chomsky, N. (2006). *Language and mind.* Cambridge: Cambridge University Press.

Clay, M. (1975). *What did I write? Beginning writing behavior.* Portsmouth, NH: Heinemann.

Collins, J. (1998). Our ideologies and theirs. In B. Schieffelin, K. Woolard & P. Kroskrity (Eds.), *Language ideologies: Practice and theory* (pp. 256–270). Oxford: Oxford University Press.

Compton-Lily, C. (2007). The complexities of reading in two Puerto Rican families. *Reading Research Quarterly, 42*, 72–98.

Cummins, J. (1984). *Bilingualism and special education: Issues in assessment and pedagogy.* San Diego, Calif.: College-Hill Press.

—— (1994). Knowledge, power, and identity in teaching English as a second language. In F. Genesee (Ed.), *Educating second language children: The whole child, the whole curriculum, the whole community* (pp. 33–58). Cambridge: Cambridge University Press.

Delgado-Gaitan, C. (1992). School matters in the Mexican-American home: Socializing children to education. *American Educational Research Journal, 29*, 495–513.

Dyson, A. H. (1993). *Social worlds of children learning to write in an urban primary school.* New York: Teachers College Press.

—— (2002). Writing and children's symbolic repertoires: Development unhinged. In S. Neuman & D. Dickinson (Eds.), *Handbook of early literacy research* (pp. 126–141). New York: Guilford Press.

Ferreiro, E. (1986). The interplay between information and assimilation in beginning literacy. In W. Teale & E. Sulzby (Eds.), *Emergent literacy: Writing and reading* (pp. 15–49). Norwood, NJ: Ablex Publishing.

Ferreiro, E., & Teberosky, A. (1982). *Literacy before schooling.* Portsmouth, NH: Heinemann.

Freire, P. (2003). *Pedagogy of the oppressed.* New York: Continuum.

Fu, D. (2003). *An island of English: Teaching ESL in Chinatown.* Portsmouth, NH: Heinemann.

Fukuda, T. (2003). *Ushiro ni iru no dare.* Tokyo: Shinfusha Publishers.

Gardner, H. (1982). *Art, mind, and brain: A cognitive approach to creativity.* New York: Basic Books.

Gee, J. P. (1996). *Social linguistics and literacies: Ideology and discourse* (2nd ed.). London: Taylor & Francis.

—— (2002). A sociocultural perspective on early literacy development. In S. Neuman & D. Dickinson (Eds.), *Handbook of early literacy research* (pp. 30–42). New York: Guilford Press.

—— (2004). Language, literacy, politics, and public education II. International Scholar's Forum. Hofstra University, November 15–16.

—— (2005). Semiotic social spaces and affinity spaces: From *The Age of Mythology* to today's schools. In D. Barton & K. Tusting (Eds.), *Beyond communities of practice: Language, power, and social context* (pp. 214–232). Cambridge: Cambridge University Press.

Genesee, F. (2000). Early bilingual language development: One language or two? In L. Wei (Ed.), *The bilingualism reader* (pp. 327–343). London and New York: Routledge.

Goffman, E. (1981). *Forms of talk.* Philadelphia, Pa.: University of Philadelphia Press.

Goodman, D., Flurkey, A., & Goodman, Y. (2007). Effective young beginning readers. In Y. Goodman & P. Martens (Eds.), *Critical issues in early literacy* (pp. 3–16). Mahwah, NJ: Lawrence Erlbaum.

Goodman, K. S. (1996). *On reading.* Portsmouth, NH: Heinemann.

Goodman, K. S., & Goodman, Y. (1990). Vygotsky in a whole language perspective. In L. Moll (Ed.), *Vygotsky and education* (pp. 223–250). Cambridge: Cambridge University Press.

Goodman, K. S., Shannon, P., Goodman, Y., & Papoport, R. (Eds.). (2004). *Saving our schools: The case for public education, saying no to "No Child Left Behind."* Berkeley, Calif.: RDR Books.

Gort, M. (2006). Strategic codeswitching, interliteracy, and other phenomena of emergent bilingual writing: Lessons from a first grade dual language classrooms. *Journal of Early Childhood Literacy, 6*, 323–354.

Greatschools. (n.d.). School overview. Available online at www.greatschools.net (accessed February 19, 2006).

Gregory, E. (1996). *Making sense of a new world: Learning to read in a second language.* London: Paul Chapman Publishing.

Gregory, E., Long, S., & Volk, D. (2004). Syncretic literacy studies: Starting points. In E. Gregory, S. Long, & D. Volk (Eds.), *Many pathways to literacy: Young children learning with siblings, grandparents, peers and communities* (pp. 1–5). London: RoutledgeFalmer.

Gutierrez, K., & Rogoff, B. (2003). Cultural ways of learning: Individual traits of repertoires of practice. *Educational Researcher, 32,* 19–25.

Hakuta, K. (1986). *Mirror of language: The debate on bilingualism.* New York: Basic Books.

Halcon, J. (2001). Mainstream ideology and literacy instruction for Spanish-speaking children. In M. de La Luz Reyes & J. J. Halcón (Eds.), *The best for our children: Critical perspectives on literacy for Latino students* (pp. 65–77). New York: Teachers College Press.

Haneda, M. (2005). Investing in foreign-language writing: A study of two multicultural learners. *Journal of Language, Identity, and Education, 4,* 269–290.

Haney, M. (2002). Name writing: A window into the emergent literacy skills of young children. *Early Childhood Education Journal, 30,* 101–105.

Hantzopoulas, M. (2005). English only? Greek language as currency in Queens, New York City. *Language, Communities, and Education, 3,* 1–6.

Harste, J. C., Woodward, V. A., & Burke, C. L. (1984). *Language stories and literacy lessons.* Portsmouth, NH: Heinemann.

Hayashi, A. (1986). *Osukisama konbawa.* Tokyo: Fukuinkan-Shoten Publishers.

Heath, S. B. (1983). *Ways with words: Language, life, and work in communities and classrooms.* Cambridge: Cambridge University Press.

Heath, S. B., & Wolf, S. (2004). *Art is all about looking: Drawing and detail.* London: Creative Partnerships.

Heller, M. (1988). Strategic ambiguity: Codeswitching in the management of conflict. In M. Heller (Ed.), *Codeswitching: Anthropological and sociolinguistic perspectives* (pp. 77–96). New York: Mouton de Gruyter.

Hildreth, G. (1936). Developmental sequences in name writing. *Child Development, 7,* 291–303.

Hoffman, E. (1989). *Lost in translation: A life in a new language.* New York: Penguin.

Holland, D., Lachicotte, W., Skinner, D., & Cain, C. (1998). *Identity and agency in cultural worlds.* Cambridge, Mass.: Harvard University Press.

Holquist, M. (Ed.) (1981). *The dialogic imagination: Four essays by M. M. Bakhtin.* Austin, Tex.: University of Texas Press.

Ivanic, R. (1988). *Writing and identity: The discoursal construction of identity in academic writing.* Philadelphia, Pa.: John Benjamins.

John-Steiner, V. (1985). *Notebooks of the mind.* Albuquerque, N. Mex.: University of New Mexico Press.

Kabuto, B. (2005). Understanding early biliteracy development through book-handling behaviors. *Talking Points, 16,* 10–15.

Kamii, C., & Manning, M. (2002). Phonemic awareness and beginning reading and writing. *Journal of Research in Childhood Education, 17,* 38–46.

Kenner, C. (2004). Living in simultaneous worlds: Difference and integration in bilingual script-learning. *Bilingual Education and Bilingualism, 7,* 43–61.

Kenner, C., & Kress, G. (2003). The multisemiotic resources of biliterate children. *Journal of Early Childhood Literacy, 3,* 179–202.

Kohn, A. (2000). *The case against standardized testing: Raising the scores, ruining the schools.* Portsmouth, NH: Heinemann.

Krashen, S. (1982). *Principles and practice in second language acquisition.* New York: Pergamon.

Kress, G. (1997). *Before writing: Rethinking the paths to literacy.* London and New York: Routledge.

Kristeva, J. (2003). Stranger to ourselves. In International Center for Photography (Ed.), *Strangers: The first ICP triennial of photography and video* (pp. 124–127). New York: Steidl.

Lave, J., & Wenger, E. (1991). *Situated learning: Legitimate peripheral participation.* Cambridge: Cambridge University Press.

Leland, C., & Harste, J. (1994). Multiple ways of knowing: Curriculum in a new key. *Language Arts, 71,* 337–345.

Lin, W.-Y. (2007). The literacy stories of Tang-Tang and Tien-Tien. In Y. Goodman & P. Martens (Eds.), *Critical issues in early literacy: Research and pedagogy* (pp. 17–30). Mahwah, NJ: Lawrence Erlbaum.

Martinez-Roldan, C., & Malave, G. (2004). Language ideologies mediating literacy and identity in bilingual context. *Journal of Early Childhood Literacy, 4*, 155–180.

Martinez-Roldan, C. & Sayer, P. (2006). Reading through linguistic borderlines: Latino students' transactions with narrative texts. *Journal of Early Childhood Literacy, 6*(3), 293–322.

Matsuno, M. (1985). *Kasa*. Tokyo: Fukuinkan Shoten.

Moje, E., & Luke, A. (2009). Literacy and identity: Examining the metaphors in history and contemporary research. *Reading Research Quarterly, 44*, 415–437.

Moll, L. (2004). Early biliteracy development: Issues from a longitudinal study. Paper presented at the Critical Issues in Early Literacy Development, University of Arizona, Tucson, Ariz.

National K-12 Foreign Language Survey (2009). Center for Applied Linguistics. Available online at http://www.cal.org/projects/flsurvey.html (accessed October 15, 2009).

Novak, M. (1996). *Elmer Blunt's open house*. New York: Scholastic.

Owocki, G. (1999). *Literacy through play*. Portsmouth, NH: Heinemann.

Owocki, G., & Goodman, Y. (2002). *Kidwatching: Documenting children's literacy development*. Portsmouth, NH: Heinemann.

Parke, T., Drury, R., Kenner, C., & Robertson, L. H. (2002). Revealing invisible worlds: Connecting the mainstream with bilingual children's home and community learning. *Journal of Early Childhood Literacy, 2*, 195–220.

Perez, B. (2004). Language, literacy, and biliteracy. In B. Perez (Ed.), *Sociocultural contexts of language and literacy* (2nd ed.) (pp. 3–24). Mahwah, NJ: Lawrence Erlbaum Associates.

Piaget, J. (1959). *The language and thought of the child*. London and New York: Routledge.

Piaget, J., & Inhelder, B. (2000). *The psychology of the child*. New York: Basic Books.

Popikko Doriru (n.d.). Tokyo: Zenkaken.

Reyes, I. (2004). Functions of code switching in schoolchildren's conversations. *Bilingual Research Journal, 28*, 77–98.

Rodriguez, R. (2004). *Hunger of memory: The education of Richard Rodriguez*. New York: Dial Press Trade.

Rogers, H. (2005). *Writing systems: A linguistic approach*. Malden, Mass.: Blackwell Publishing.

Rogoff, B. (2003). *The cultural nature of human development*. Oxford: Oxford University Press.

Rogoff, B., & Gardner, W. (1984). Adult guidance of cognitive development. In B. Rogoff & J. Lave (Eds.), *Everyday cognition: Development in social context* (pp. 95–116). Cambridge, Mass.: Harvard University Press.

Romaine, S. (1995). *Bilingualism*. Oxford: Blackwell.

Sassoon, R. (1995). *The acquisition of a second writing system*. Oxford: Cromwell Press.

Schieffelin, B., Woolard, K., & Paul, K. (Eds.). (1998). *Language ideologies: Practice and theory*. Oxford: Oxford University Press.

Sfard, A., & Prusak, A. (2005). Telling identities: In search of an analytic tool for investigating learning as a culturally shaped activity. *Educational Researcher, 34*, 14–22.

Shaywitz, S. (2003). *Overcoming dyslexia: A new and complete science-based program for reading problems at any level*. New York: Alfred A. Knopf.

Shimajiro (2005). Minamikata: Benesse Corporation.

Smith, F. (1994). *Understanding reading: A psycholinguistic analysis of reading and learning to read*. Hillsdale, NJ: L. Erlbaum.

Spitulnik, D. (1998). Mediating unity and diversity: The production of language ideologies in Zambian broadcasting. In B. Schieffelin, K. Woolard & K. Paul (Eds.), *Language ideologies: Practice and theory*. Oxford: Oxford University Press.

Strauss, S. (2005). *The linguistics, neurology, and politics of phonics: Silent "E" speaks out*. Mahwah, NJ: Lawrence Erlbaum.

Street, B. (2000). Literacy events and literacy practices: Theory and practice in the New Literacy Studies. In M. Martin-Jones & K. Jones (Eds.), *Multilingual literacies: Reading and writing different worlds* (pp. 17–29). Amsterdam: John Benjamins Publishing Company.

Street, J. C., & Street, B. V. (1991). The schooling of literacy. In D. Barton & R. Ivanic (Eds.), *Writing in the community* (Vol. VI, pp. 143–166). London: Sage.

Tabors, P., & Snow, C. (2002). Young bilingual children and early literacy development. In S. Neuman (Ed.), *David Dickinson* (pp. 159–178). New York: Guilford Press.

Taylor, D. (1983). *Family literacy: Young children learning to read and write*. Portsmouth, NH: Heinemann.

—— (2005). Resisting the new word order: Conceptualizing freedom in contradictory symbolic spaces. *Anthropology in Education Quarterly, 36*, 341–353.

—— (2009). Learning to read as complex traumatic experience: A re-analysis of the ethnographic data using research on cultural and psychological trauma. National Council of Teachers of English National Conference, Philadelphia, Pa.: November 19–24.

Taylor, D., Kabuto, B., MacAuthor, A., & Trujillo, L. (2002). Writing pictures, painting stories: Exploring the (symbolic) spaces in which we live our lives. *School Talk, 7*, 1–6.

Taylor, D., & Yamasaki, T. (2006). Children, literacy, and mass trauma: Teaching in times of catastrophic events and ongoing emergency situations. *GSE Perspectives on Urban Education, 4*, available online at www.urbanedjournal.org (accessed April 4, 2006).

Thompson, R. (2006). Bilingual, bicultural, and binominal identities: Personal name investment and the imagination in the lives of Korean Americans. *Journal of Language, Identity, and Education, 5*, 179–208.

Tollefson, J. (1991). *Planning language, planning inequality*. New York: Longman.

Toohey, K. (2000). *Learning English at school: Identity, social relations and classroom practice*. Buffalo, NY: Multilingual Matters Ltd.

US Census Bureau (2006). Quick Facts. Available online at www.quickfacts.census.gov (accessed October 2006).

Vygotsky, L. (1986). *Thought and language*. Cambridge, Mass.: MIT Press.

Wei, L. (1999). The "why" and "how" questions in the analysis of conversational code-switching. In P. Auer (Ed.), *Code-switching in conversation* (pp. 156–176). London and New York: Routledge.

—— (2000). Dimensions of bilingualism. In L. Wei (Ed.), *The bilingualism reader* (pp. 3–25). London and New York: Routledge.

Wenger, E. (1998). *Communities of practice: Learning, meaning, and identity*. Cambridge: Cambridge University Press.

Wertsch, J. (1991). *Voices of the mind*. Hemel Hempstead: Harvester Wheatsheaf.

Whitehead, A. N. (1925). *Science and the modern world*. New York: The Free Press.

—— (1929). *The aims of education and other essays*. New York: The Free Press.

Williams, S. (1989). *I went walking*. New York: Voyager Books.

Wilson, F. (1998). *The hand*. New York: Vintage Books.

Wood, A. (1994). *Silly Sally*. Orlando, Fla.: Harcourt Brace.

Woolard, K. (1998). Language ideology as a field of inquiry. In B. Schieffelin, K. Woolard, & K. Paul (Eds.), *Language ideologies: Practice and theory* (pp. 3–47). Oxford: Oxford University Press.

Index